'*A Matter of Life and Death* provides thought-provoking reflections from a wide range of people whose lives have been deeply influenced by encounters with dying, death and loss. Their insights into these sensitive, often taboo, subjects are inspirational and uplifting – highly recommended reading for all who work in end of life or bereavement care.'

– *Dr Marilyn Relf, Bereavement Care Lead, Sir Michael Sobell House, Oxford and Chair, National Bereavement Alliance (UK)*

'Dying conjures many stories, many feelings, many fears. Rosalind Bradley brings together the thoughts of the eminent, the well-trained and also those who have personal experience with the dying. These stories explore the inspiring, the meaningful and sometimes troubled ideas that everyone will have about death.'

– *Professor Richard Chye, University of Notre Dame Australia*

'A thoughtful collection of personal stories and perspectives on death as a defining part of life. Beautifully told and cleverly presented. A unique offering on an ultimate truth – you will be inspired, intrigued, informed and touched by the diversity and authenticity of the contributions.'

– *Professor Christine Bennett AO, Dean of Medicine, University of Notre Dame Australia*

a matter of life and death

of related interest

Final Chapters
Writings About the End of Life
Edited by Roger Kirkpatrick
Foreword by Jonathan Dimbleby
ISBN 978 1 84905 490 4
eISBN 978 0 85700 886 2

The Forgiveness Project
Stories for a Vengeful Age
Marina Cantacuzino
Forewords by Archbishop Emeritus Desmond Tutu and
Alexander McCall Smith
ISBN 978 1 84905 566 6
eISBN 978 1 78450 006 1

a matter of
life and death

60
VOICES SHARE THEIR WISDOM

ROSALIND BRADLEY

FOREWORD BY
ARCHBISHOP EMERITUS DESMOND TUTU

Jessica Kingsley *Publishers*
London and Philadelphia

For copyright acknowledgements, please see pages 15–18.

Disclaimer: Every effort has been made to trace copyright holders and to obtain their permission for the use of copyright material. The author and the publisher apologise for any omissions and would be grateful if notified of any acknowledgements that should be incorporated in future reprints or editions of this book.

First published in 2016
by Jessica Kingsley Publishers
73 Collier Street
London N1 9BE, UK
and
400 Market Street, Suite 400
Philadelphia, PA 19106, USA

www.jkp.com

Copyright © Rosalind Bradley 2016
Foreword copyright © 2015 by Desmond M. Tutu
Therese Schroeder-Sheker's contribution copyright © Therese Schroeder-Sheker 2016

Front cover image source: Shutterstock®. The cover image is for illustrative purposes only, and any person featuring is a model.

Library of Congress Cataloging in Publication Data
A CIP catalog record for this book is available from the Library of Congress

British Library Cataloguing in Publication Data
A CIP catalogue record for this book is available from the British Library

ISBN 978 1 84905 601 4
eISBN 978 1 78450 283 6

Printed and bound in Great Britain

To my dear parents Margaret and Bob Manser
and stepmother Norma Manser

Thank you for your wisdom, love and trust.

Death is not extinguishing the light;
it is only putting out the lamp
because the dawn has come.

Rabindranath Tagore

Contents

Foreword

In my twilight years I have found myself thinking more and more about my death. Strengthened by faith and a long and purposeful life, I am not frightened of dying. My life has seen many encounters with death, the anticipated and the unexpected. The question that lingers for us all is how to make sense of death when it comes. There are no easy answers. However, Dag Hammarskjöld's words resonate deeply: *Do not seek death. Death will find you. But seek the road which makes death a fulfilment.* I have come to realise that death is indeed part of my life.

I rejoice that death has become less of a taboo subject in our conversations. In this timely book you will discover precious wisdom and heartfelt insights from people from all walks of life. We hear from those who engage with death professionally on a daily basis, those whose lives have been rudely shattered by the sudden loss of a loved one and from those who gently remind us of how their faith may bring an understanding to the circle of life.

As I have listened to these voices, I have found reassurance and enlightenment. I know this book will offer the same gifts to you whether you believe in a transition to a new life or contemplate the beyond with some uncertainty. I commend it highly.

Archbishop Emeritus Desmond Tutu

Copyright Acknowledgements

With grateful thanks to the following for permission to use their work:

- Page 27, Machado, A. (2003) Translated by Berg, M. and Maloney D. *There is no road*. In A. Machado *There is No Road*. Buffalo, NY: White Pine Press. Used with permission.
- Page 30, 'Last Post', copyright © Carol Ann Duffy. Reproduced by permission of the author c/o Rogers, Coleridge and White Ltd., 20 Powis Mews, London W11 1JN.
- Page 31, Kemp, R. *Everyone a Hero* [excerpt]. Message given at Andrew Griffiths' memorial service. Used with permission.
- Page 40, **UK:** Blessing: 'For the Dying'. From *Benedictus* by John O'Donohue. Published by Bantam Press. Reprinted by permission of The Random House Group Limited.
- Page 40, **USA:** Blessing: 'For the Dying'. From *To Bless the Space Between Us: A Book of Blessings* by John O'Donohue, copyright © 2008 by John O'Donohue. Used by permission of Doubleday, an imprint of the Knopf Doubleday Publishing Group, a division of Penguin Random House LLC. All rights reserved.
- Page 43, *Walking on the Pastures of Wonder*. © John Quinn, Estate of John O'Donohue. Veritas Publications, 2015. Used with permission.
- Page 46, Green, J. *An Abundance of Katherines*. Published by the Penguin Group. Used with permission.
- Page 52, Sheila Kitzinger. *Women's Experience of Sex*. London: Dorling Kindersley. Used with permission of her husband Uwe Kitzinger and daughter Tess McKenney.
- Pages 55–56, Shipp, K. (2014) Email sent to Kinny Gardiner. Used with permission.
- Page 58, Excerpt(s) from *When Bad Things Happen to Good People* by Harold S. Kushner, copyright © 1981 by Harold S. Kushner. Used by permission of Schocken Books, an imprint of the Knopf Doubleday Publishing Group, a division of Penguin Random House LLC. All rights reserved.
- Page 58, Mendel, M., Rabbi of Rymanov (2002) 'Human beings are God's language.' In preface H.S. Kushner, *When Bad Things Happen to Good People*. London: Pan Books. Rabbi Mendel (1745–1815) was a Hasidic master.

Acknowledgements

Many people assisted me with compiling this book. Their wise words, encouragement and feedback have all been very much appreciated. I would like to give special thanks to Alex Nelson and Liz McCarthy for their constant creative listening and valuable editorial advice which they generously offered throughout the preparation of this book.

My twin brother Martin Manser, editor *par excellence*, made himself available throughout the whole process, answering queries and offering reassurance. Dr Marilyn Relf also gave me helpful advice and suggestions for which I am very grateful.

I received many constructive responses about the draft manuscript from friends and colleagues: Diana Baird, Professor Christine Bennett AO, Rob Brennan, Betty Carmody, Fr Daven Day SJ, Jennifer Gribble, Paul Hoffman, Dennis Hunter-Papp, Pam Masini, Bridget McKern, Ben Quinn, Jorie Ryan, Terese Sheridan, Megan Warrell and Wendy Wright.

I also received suggestions for potential contributors or helpful comments from: James Alison, Marcus Bower, Chris Boylan, Canteen Australia, Sally Charkos, Ven. Robina Courtin, Ven. Thubten Chokyi, Judith Daley, Kerry de Waal, Gill Green, Heather Green, Sherry Gregory, Christopher Hall, Renée Hayden, Charlie Hogg, Judith and Miriam Ish-Horowicz, Peta Keaney, Lis Long, Norma Manser,

Walter Mason, Leon Milroy, Don Pereira, Neville Roach AO, Herman Roborgh, Frances Rush, Karen Shipp, Revd Austin Smith, Josefine Speyer, Reverend Helen Summers, Judi Taylor, Sharne Thomas, Julie Tregarthen, Linda Turton, Michele White, Richard White and The Reverend Jonathan Woodhouse CB.

Thank you to others who have played their part in making this book come to fruition: Tim Barnes, Julie Crawford, Trevor Dalziell, Bethany Gower and colleagues at JKP, Penny Hunt, Sue Mason from Ashgate Hospicecare and Kathy Pereira.

I am immensely grateful to Archbishop Emeritus Desmond Tutu who generously wrote the foreword to this book.

Finally, a thousand thanks to my husband Steve and three children for their love and patience while I spent countless hours at the computer.

Introduction

Death is natural, part of our human existence and a great equaliser. For many people, it is a sacred end to their lives. Nevertheless, death remains a mystery. What happens when we die? Why do we die? What dies when we die? Is there life after death?

How do we respond to these very human but existential questions? Do we keep them to ourselves? Or do we discuss them with other people and, if so, with whom?

Although answers to these major questions lie beyond our understanding, I hope this book will suggest some insights into this subject. In the following pages, people from many walks of life share their wisdom and perspectives as they face up to end-of-life issues. Their reflections may help dispel some of the fears that surround death and dying, and will also, I hope, encourage us to speak out more on this often avoided and delicate subject.

A Matter of Life and Death presents a compilation of inspiring verses, images and reflections. It is a resource to dip into, intended for those who are ageing, those suffering a terminal illness at any age, those who care for the sick and dying, and those trying to make sense of life and death. Chaplains, celebrants, grief counsellors, pastoral care teams, nursing and medical personnel may find resonance with their work with the dying and the bereaved.

Each contributor to this book treats death with respect and dignity. Many acknowledge the paradox of living and dying. Together with the accompanying feelings of pain, fear, anger and deep sorrow, they recognise that death can also bring a healing, a sense of peace, a meaning to life and sometimes a spiritual awakening or a strengthening of spirit. Death is *here* in our midst and *there* beyond our physical realm. Death comes to meet us anticipated or not. Sometimes it finds us ready and waiting; sometimes it's a surprise and even a shock.

A recurrent theme in the contributions is the importance of preparing for death while continuing to live fully and courageously. Facing death realistically by being grateful for our lives, letting go of past disappointments, forgiving others and ourselves, and taking care of practical family concerns may help loosen death's stranglehold on us. Recognising that death lies beyond our chronology means that at some point we hand over the baton to future generations. This may then help us to become more emotionally and spiritually prepared for death and so lead more fulfilled lives in the present.

A Matter of Life and Death has five parts. In *Personal Encounters with Death*, contributors share how their lives have been reshaped in the aftermath of a gradual dying or a sudden death. In *Death Brings Us Wisdom*, contributors express deep insights about death and how it affects our daily living. *Working Closely with Death* follows those who engage with death on a daily basis, and considers how they cope with and understand this subject. *Death and the Circle of Life* explores how death is part of our natural life cycle, and *Death Is Sacred* presents multicultural and multifaith views of death.

The contributors have opened their hearts and souls to share their personal reflections on this sensitive and intimate subject. It has been a privilege to receive their emails as we worked together. I asked them to choose a passage or image that expressed death to them, together with their personal reflections on their choice, based on their spiritual inclination or an experience with death. I hope that their collective wisdom, together with the further verses at the end of each part that inspired me during my research, will resonate with you.

People often ask what prompted me to undertake this book. The seed was sown by my mother's sudden death while she was staying with us in Australia, on holiday (from England). It was a few days after 11 September 2001. One day we were strolling around the Sydney Opera House, the next day she was in an emergency department following a cardiac arrest. I can still recall the physical and emotional numbness I felt that day and for many months afterwards.

Then, several years later, when two close friends who were siblings died, I felt even more driven to come to terms with my own mortality and face up to my own death, my own fears and how I wanted to live the rest of my life. Exploring the mystery of death in all its rawness and complexity and gleaning some meaning from it led me to create *A Matter of Life and Death*. Inviting these diverse contributors to participate has made me deeply aware that death is very much part of our lives.

The contributors to this book have taught me to think differently about death as well as about living. Journeying with this book has encouraged me to live a fuller and more authentic life, and one without regrets. I am more sensitive to the need to take care of my relationships, not to leave the love unsaid and to spend some time in daily reflection and meditation. As I grow older, it has also led me to ponder what matters most to me and to consider communicating my end-of-life wishes, including advance care planning. I am now more confident about discussing death with family and friends. It has been a rich and rewarding time.

As you read through or dip into this book, my hope is that your sense of your own mortality will be deepened, and that you will become more comfortable talking honestly about death with others. Coming to terms with death can enrich the meaning of our lives once we become fully conscious that our lifespan is limited and we learn to live more in the present. I believe that death is a natural transition from one stage of consciousness to another. As one contributor neatly put it, 'death is a comma, not a full stop'. Whether you accept that premise or not, the fact remains that we are all in transit and need to face up to the reality of our own death. How we deal with that realisation is at the heart of this book.

Rosalind Bradley, December 2015
www.rosbradley.com

Postscript

All royalties from this book will go to Ashgate Hospicecare, Derbyshire, UK, where Deborah Loeb, a dear friend, chose to spend her final days. I was present at Deborah's initial cancer diagnosis in late 2007 and felt with her in the closing stages of her life. Deborah died in February 2008, and I wanted to honour her life and pay my respects to the staff who looked after her with great compassion and grace during her final weeks. (See page 221 for more information.)

PART I

Personal Encounters with Death

In Part 1, a diverse range of contributors share how their lives have been shattered and reshaped in the aftermath of a gradual dying or a sudden death. Death comes to meet us anticipated or not. The fear, shock, despair, rage and sorrow of death are all acknowledged alongside the many powerful and complex forces that surround this subject: its transformative experience, the resilience of the human spirit and how death is as much a process as life itself.

Contributors include an army brigadier whose son was wounded in action and later died; a Holocaust survivor whose mother died moments after surviving the Second World War; a physiotherapist whose eminent surgeon husband and son died within two years of each other; a mother who, while working in child bereavement, lost her daughter to cancer; a mental health professor who is dedicated to suicide prevention; a prisoner on death row whose life has been transformed through Buddhism; a minister who knew he was dying; a former Indian diplomat who found it hard to accept the death of his father; a performance artist who grieves for his late husband; a sister who co-founded a peace organisation after her brother was killed in the 9/11 attacks; a mother who, in the wake of losing her baby son, works in the field of bereavement; and two teenagers who are coping with the loss of one or both parents.

Their sentiments include:

'This is where I unite with my husband
and son on a soul level.'

'I don't live in the past; the past lives in me.'

'At times I have felt a hidden and
mysterious ally beyond myself...'

'...don't leave love unsaid.'

'This is our living forfeit.'

Gail O'Brien

*Non-Executive Director, Chris O'Brien
Lifehouse; physiotherapist*

AUSTRALIA

Traveler, your footprints
are the only road, nothing else.
Traveler, there is no road;
you make your own path as you walk.
As you walk, you make your own road,
and when you look back
you see the path
you will never travel again.
Traveler, there is no road
only a ship's wake on the sea.

Antonio Machado, *There is No Road*

We are all beset by crises of varying degrees of gravity, and our family was no different. In 2009, Chris, a father and internationally renowned surgeon, died from brain cancer. Less than two years later, Adam, our eldest son, aged 28, developed epilepsy and, one Saturday morning, a final seizure took his life. Then, in 2012, my beautiful 28-year-old daughter was diagnosed with cancer. Her treatment was immensely challenging but her prognosis is good and she is now well.

These three traumatic family events in close succession were a lot to process but they have provided me with an opportunity to search for meaning in life and death. This passage by Antonio Machado resonates deeply. It has induced my reflection on the intersecting and circuitous

27

nature of life. Looking back, I can now see how the dots have joined forming the path I have travelled.

The process has not been one of contemplative philosophising. Rather, it has been a punishing journey, sometimes manic, sometimes foolish and dangerous, trying to grasp where my loved ones have gone and why this has happened. Through this, I have found spirituality, hope and purpose in my life.

I have faith in a divine order and a transcendent, transformative spirituality. Through Christianity, and far beyond, to the divine cosmic consciousness where there are no more tears, I have found peace. I have stopped searching for answers outside myself, and go with the flow and trust my inner voice. This is where I unite with my husband and son on a soul level. It is where I came from and where I will return to without fear and regret after completing this earthly journey.

About 13 years ago, I converted to Catholicism. I was drawn to the physical and visual expression of spirituality in the Catholic Church, the sense of celebration, the intensity of the Eucharist, the invocation of the sacred at the Easter masses and the sense of peace and community in our parish, affectionately called Villa Maria, where I sing in our little choir.

The inner work of contemplation and meditation is a powerful and nourishing healing tool and has become a daily practice to allow the spirit to come in. I have found this to be the path to mental resilience, self-knowledge and healing, and to understanding life and death as part of the same process, all One.

I ponder the idea that God is the process of life itself, and that we are indeed one body, one Lord of all, the visible and the invisible, all that is seen and unseen, light from light, true God from true God. We are all an instrument of the Divine. Each day I ask for guidance, to be a channel of grace and an instrument of joy, peace, humility, knowledge and, most importantly, gratitude.

Before he died, Chris and I dreamed of creating a holistic and comprehensive cancer centre at the Royal Prince Alfred Hospital (RPA) in Sydney where he worked. After his death, I was determined his dream would become a reality. Chris O'Brien Lifehouse opened at Royal Prince Alfred Hospital in 2013 to give people hope and peace on their cancer journey.

* * *

Gail O'Brien is a physiotherapist and a Non-Executive Director of the Chris O'Brien Lifehouse, a holistic and comprehensive cancer centre, based in Sydney, Australia (www.mylifehouse.org.au). Gail was widowed in 2009. Gail uses her own experience and insights to encourage and inspire others on the cancer journey and talk about the new hope that lies ahead for the many Australians who each year are diagnosed with cancer.

Brigadier Michael Griffiths CBE

*Retired army officer, Duke of Lancaster's
Regiment; police officer*

UK

My son, Captain Andrew Griffiths, was wounded in action by an explosion while leading his soldiers on an operation in the Helmand province of Afghanistan in August 2010. Twelve days later, surrounded by his family, Andrew died of his wounds at the Queen Elizabeth Hospital, Birmingham.

In my grief, I have turned to three passages, which reflect the various moods I find myself slipping into when things get tough. My first is the poem 'Last Post' by poet laureate Dame Carol Ann Duffy. For me, this poem reflects that 'bargaining' phase of grief when all you want to do is put things back as they were. I probably stayed in that place for far too long, willing every day that somehow this was all just a horrible dream. That it was me who was somewhere else. Her concluding line – 'If poetry could truly tell it backwards, then it would' – holds deep meaning for me.

For several years we kept his helmet and rucksack at the foot of our bed so that upon waking we returned to face the reality of the place we were really in. We so want one last chance to talk to him, to hear his voice, to feel his great big arms around our shoulders. We just want him back in a way that sometimes makes us feel ill, and yet, in our rational times, we know that we cannot have any of these things – just memories, which seem such little compensation for all that we have lost.

This really is the 'if only' part of my life and with it sometimes comes a frustration and an impotence that for all my faith, for all my belief and for all that I had achieved, none of this was enough to give Andrew what he needed most at that time – life. And yet I know that in thinking like this, I end up questioning my faith, which in turn questions the basis on which we do so much in God's name. It is something I wrestle with on a daily basis.

The second piece is by Colonel Richard Kemp titled 'Everyone a Hero'. Its focus is on the sacrifices that the war dead gave in the service of their country. In this extract, the words speak to what they have forfeited by dying.

> They forfeited their every hope and every dream. Every laugh and every tear. Every tender moment with the girl they married or the girl they might have married. Every smile from a beloved son or daughter… Every beer enjoyed with friends. Every game of rugby played or watched… The exhilaration of every achievement, the frustration of every setback, the sorrow of every failure.
>
> Colonel Richard Kemp, *Everyone a Hero*

I know every 'early' death brings out this reaction – the many 'what ifs' and what might have been. Andrew lived his life at pace and did not want to waste a minute. He had a great life, and our hearts and minds are filled with many wonderful memories of him and his exploits, but any life as good as his had so much more to offer. I know we were so lucky to have him and, almost as a consequence, our lives are so much worse off without him. As time moves on, so life moves on; wonderful family events happen but there is always someone now missing from that enjoyment and we all quietly and privately endure that desperate ache. As one of our daughters said recently, 'Our lives have and will always have an Andrew-sized hole in them.' This is our living forfeit.

The final passage is from President Theodore Roosevelt. It spells out to me what drives those young men and women knowingly and willingly to commit acts of selfless bravery in the service of their country.

> The credit belongs to the man who is actually in the arena, whose face is marred by dust and sweat and blood; who strives valiantly; who errs, who comes short again and again…who spends himself in a worthy cause; who at the best knows in the end the triumph of high achievement… so that his place shall never be with those cold and timid souls who neither know victory nor defeat.

President Theodore Roosevelt, *The Man in the Arena*

These words have a very personal resonance. Andrew simply never gave up. He was so strong and determined. He was such a great example to all of us, and his memory continues to challenge us to this day. The stories of him immediately after being blown up are simply inspiring. Checking that no one else had been hurt, continuing to issue orders, making jokes with his blokes as they dealt with his wounds and finally saying thank you to his platoon sergeant as he placed him on the CASEVAC [casualty evacuation] helicopter. Despite his grievous wounds, Andrew fought so hard to get home to say goodbye to us. I think of that immense strength and determination often when I succumb to sadness and self-pity.

These three pieces give some sense to what I might be feeling at any given time. So often I still believe this is all a nightmare and then imagine what I might do *if only* things could go back to what they were; sometimes they remind me what he and we have lost for all time, and when I question *why*, I need to remind myself that Andrew lived to be in that 'arena'.

* * *

Mike Griffiths recently retired from the Army after a career of 35 years. He was commissioned into the Infantry aged 19 and left in the rank of brigadier after service in Northern Ireland, Cyprus, Bosnia and Afghanistan. In his last years, he was Colonel of the Duke of Lancaster's Regiment, the regiment that his son Andrew joined in 2008.

Olga Horak OAM

Holocaust survivor; volunteer Survivor Guide, Sydney Jewish Museum

AUSTRALIA

> Forgetfulness leads to exile and remembering is the key to redemption.
>
> Israel Baal Shem Tov

'I don't live in the past; the past lives in me' is what I tell visitors at the Sydney Jewish Museum. When I was in Auschwitz-Birkenau and Bergen-Belsen, I constantly saw death. Smelt it and tasted it. Before coming to Auschwitz, I had never seen a dead body, but here we saw death every waking moment. It was as common as breathing. I came from Czechoslovakia, a cultured society where people usually died from sickness or old age. Here, death was murder cruelly inflicted upon us.

I have defeated death many times. Twice I 'passed' selection by the notorious SS officer Dr Josef Mengele, both times in Auschwitz. This may have been unusual but I felt it was also a triumph. Yes, I did wonder why I was spared. Why me? Why was I chosen by G-d? Although I was young, I did not feel especially lucky, but I did feel strongly (and still do) that I have a moral duty to teach people the truth of what happened to the millions of innocent Jewish people who were systematically persecuted, rounded up and transported to death camps.

I believe that this is my mission in life and this gets me out of bed every morning, although I am now in my late eighties. I endeavour to teach truth in order to develop spiritual and moral strength, so that people of different cultures can live in harmony. I am grateful that my grandchildren understand that they are the last living link to a Holocaust survivor and they too have responsibilities.

When my mother collapsed and died moments after registering as a survivor, I did not think I would survive. I was heartbroken. Together, we had survived Auschwitz, a death march from Kurzbach to Dresden, the journey to Bergen-Belsen and four months in the 'cesspool' there, only for her to die just after she registered as a survivor. I had lost my mother forever and I was now completely alone. This moment still haunts me. I tried to find her the following day but she had no name or marker, nothing to distinguish her from the thousands of other bodies lying around the camps. I felt an enormous sense of guilt that I lived while my mother lay somewhere unknown in this horrendous hellhole. I still carry the pain of this loss today.

I speak too of the dangers of hatred. Not everyone was evil and there were examples of kindness and humanity. Strangers took me in after the war, gradually nursing me back to a semblance of health before I travelled home to Bratislava. Here my life changed – I met my future husband and we moved to Australia to start a new life. As my children grew up, my story slowly unfolded. At first, I was very shy about telling my story, but now it is hard to keep me quiet.

Every month, I teach nurses how to offer appropriate care for Holocaust survivors living in nursing homes. Memories of camp horrors often return as survivors age; they become scared of uniforms, receiving orders or being treated as a number. Gentleness and softness are necessary.

Suicides were uncommon in Auschwitz. Despite the terrible fear and pain we all suffered, there was a primal urge to live, hope and survive. I am not scared of death myself.

The Holocaust was a turning point in history that prompted the world to say 'never again'. I pray that will be so.

*** *** ***

Olga Horak was the only member of her family to survive the Holocaust. Her mother died moments after she registered as a survivor in 1945 at Bergen-Belsen. Olga started a new life in Australia with her husband, John, and was one of the first volunteer Survivor Guides when the Sydney Jewish Museum opened in 1992 (www.sydneyjewishmuseum. com.au). Her autobiography, *Auschwitz to Australia*, was published in 2000.

Editor's postscript

Australian war artist Lieutenant Alan Moore, aged 30, entered Bergen-Belsen in 1945 and courageously sketched and photographed the corpses, the starved and the diseased, forever haunted by what he saw. His diary entry mentions an 18-year-old girl in the infirmary called Olga Rosenberger who weighed 29kg and was close to death. He often wondered what happened to her.

In 2005 the Sydney Jewish Museum approached Alan for the loan of some paintings and photographs for an exhibition, *Through Australian Eyes*, to commemorate the 60th anniversary of the liberation of Bergen-Belsen. Alan asked if anyone knew of a lady called Olga Rosenberger; he had no idea if she was still alive or where she might be. Olga Horak (née Rosenberger) was indeed alive and an active volunteer guide at the museum. Olga and Alan met again at the Sydney Jewish Museum: a touching moment for them both. Alan celebrated his 100th birthday in August 2014, his intellect still sharp and intact.

Olga Horak and Alan Moore, together after 60 years at a reunion on Victory in Europe (VE) Day at the Australian Holocaust Museum, Sunday 8 May 2005

Photo: Lisa Wiltse/Fairfax Syndication

Colleen Kelly

*Co-founder, September 11th Families
for Peaceful Tomorrows*

USA

If I should ever leave you whom I love
To go along the silent way,
Grieve not, nor speak of me with tears,
But laugh and talk of me as if I were beside you, for
Who knows, but that I shall be oftentimes?

I'd come – I'd come, could I but find a way!
But would not tears and grief be barriers?
And when you hear a song I used to sing,
Or see a bird I loved,
let not the thought of me be sad
For I am loving you just as I always have
You were so good to me!

So many things I wanted still to do
So many, many things to say to you
Remember that I did not fear
It was just leaving you I could not bear to face.
We cannot see beyond, but this I know;
I loved you so – 'twas heaven here with you!

Isla P. Richardson, *To Those I Love*

I had seen a shorter version of Richardson's beautiful poem on many funeral Mass cards, but it was not until after my brother's death on 9/11 that I read the full passage. Her words still resonate true for the following reasons:

Because I was relentlessly haunted by the question of whether my brother was terrified during his final moments. This poem gives me hope that he was not.

Because the poem urges all of us to speak from our hearts every day; don't leave love unsaid.

Because the poem describes heaven as here on earth, and integrally connected to love.

And lastly, because I believe death is as much a process as new life.

Just as it takes nine months from conception until birth, I believe death is also a process that lingers for months. I could 'feel' my brother's presence on many an occasion after he died. I like to believe he *was* and *is* beside me oftentimes and that gives me great comfort.

* * *

Colleen Kelly is a Roman Catholic in her bones and a Quaker at heart. Her brother, Bill Kelly Jr, was killed in the 9/11 attacks, while attending a conference at the World Trade Center. Colleen later co-founded September 11th Families for Peaceful Tomorrows, an organisation dedicated to nonviolent and just response to the violence in our world (www.peacefultomorrows.org).

In 2011, Colleen received the Pax Christi USA Teacher Award.

Professor Patrick McGorry AO

Professor of Youth Mental Health, University of Melbourne; Australian of the Year 2010

AUSTRALIA

May there be some beautiful surprise
Waiting for you inside death,
Something you never knew or felt,
Which with one simple touch
Absolves you of all loneliness and loss,
As you quicken within the embrace
For which your soul was eternally made.

John O'Donohue, *For the Dying*

The mystery of death and the powerful and complex forces that surround it were first revealed to me when my mother and my grandmother died on the same day in 1991. My maternal grandmother, Sheila, aged 91, a formidable woman and medical doctor, was terminally ill with lung cancer, and was in hospital in Newcastle, Australia. She and my mother, Margaret, had a complex relationship and had lived on opposite sides of the world until my father's death four years earlier.

My mother was in fact more disabled with heart disease and cardiac failure. Since my father's death, she had come out of her shell, after living most of her life in the shadow of both her mother's and her husband's strong personalities. I was planning to return to Newcastle on a Friday, as I knew my grandmother was dying, but fatefully put it off for 24 hours due to work pressures, always my Achilles heel in life.

The next morning my mother received a phone call from the hospital to inform her that her mother had just died. It appears that soon after receiving this news she herself had a cardiac arrest. When a friend called round, she found her unconscious. It was not possible to revive her, and within a matter of minutes my mother and grandmother were both gone.

The next days were surreal, with a numbing flight home followed by a double funeral. I will always feel terribly guilty for not having been there that Saturday morning as planned. I believe that, as a doctor, I might have been able to prevent or at least postpone my mother's death. An additional deep sadness was linked to the complexity of the double tragedy of their deaths and their unhappiness during their final years, and especially for the elusive freedom never realised by my mother. One lesson I drew was that while there may have been a rational explanation for the events, it was insufficient. Higher forces were involved. Irish mystic and philosopher John O'Donohue is a comforting guide to dealing with separation, loss and death. His words embrace those who, on their deathbed, are haunted by regret for their unlived life.

Six years later, my younger brother, Hugh, aged 37, died of liver failure, caused by severe alcoholism, which eventually destroyed him physically, mentally and spiritually. This all too common curse had seriously threatened several other members of my close family, but through their courage, and, I believe, the exquisite hand of divine intercession, they had survived the threat of premature death and, in many ways, had flourished. Bullets had been dodged in fearful yet incredible ways. But words will never be able to express the depth of my gratitude that two other close family members were later spared my brother's fate. At some level, I felt it was divine intervention.

All my professional career I have worked with young people whose intense and lonely struggle with mental suffering weakens their life force and allows the shadow of death to prematurely fall upon them. In Australia, hundreds, and worldwide, millions, of young people succumb every year, and many more older people too. Suicide is a massive waste of human potential; it inflicts unbearable and relentless suffering upon parents, close family and friends. Some years ago, I came into contact with a group of parents bereaved through the suicide of their adolescent and young adult children. This experience more profoundly awakened me to the endless horror of this most destructive of all modes of death and I felt much more compelled to fight this early invasion of death at every level.

The year 2014 was a shocking exception, as, with mounting budget cuts to our staffing and with team morale in free fall, we lost eight young people to suicide within a matter of months. In the wider Victorian mental health system, also subject to severe cuts, over 350 patients died prematurely from preventable deaths, mostly suicide. Three young trainee psychiatrists also suicided. Unprecedented. Death was on the rampage. Reactions varied. Some felt the loss and failure intensely yet were paralysed by impotent rage and despair. I felt that rage too, especially because I know that these deaths are nearly always preventable. That knowledge is based on sound research evidence and long experience. It is essential for me to reject despair and to help sustain myself, and my colleagues, to fight without compromise on all fronts to stop these deaths.

As a clinician and as a human being, I have been immersed in the struggle between these powerful and obscure forces of life and death. Yet I have often experienced decisive and subtle shifts in fortune that I cannot explain, but can sense and feel. I am left with a feeling of awe and gratitude when this happens. We have many weapons, medical, psychological, social, cultural and political, that we can amass and deploy. Perhaps the most powerful of these is our personal relationship with and commitment to the endangered ones. From this wide array of weapons, it is possible for us to save individual lives, and indirectly those of so many people we have not even met. The power of the social group and the community is also strong. We need to mobilise these weapons and develop new ones.

At times I have felt a hidden and mysterious ally beyond myself in relation to my patients, my own family and even the many Australians who have reached out in desperation to me in recent years to ask for help. I am convinced that a higher power is deeply involved in this mission to preserve and extend lives and that this power seems to lie partly within and work through us.

Death is with us throughout our lives and comes to us all. It is a source of deep anxiety for many of us. The challenge for me, having fought against premature death on a daily basis, is how to overcome this existential fear of death and develop an acceptance or even a welcoming mind-set. In *Walking on the Pastures of Wonder*, John O'Donohue notes that 'Death is the unseen companion, the unknown companion who walks every step of the journey with us...' He goes on to argue that, in unifying all that has happened in one's life and a reunification with all those one has loved, 'Death in that sense is a time of great homecoming, and there is no need to be afraid'.

As the Connemara Irish say, '*Ní feidir dul i bhfholach ar an mbás*' – you cannot hide from death.

* * *

Professor Patrick McGorry was born in Ireland and emigrated to Australia as a teenager in the late 1960s. Married with three sons, he is Professor of Youth Mental Health at the University of Melbourne. His professional interests are in youth mental health, early intervention for emerging serious mental ill-health and mental health reform. Patrick was Australian of the Year in 2010.

The Burton–Gaudiosi Family

Mother of four young children, Sonia Burton lost her husband Mark to melanoma in 2012. Her eldest child Tamika, then aged 12, played baseball, and when teammate Bella Gaudiosi lost her father from a sudden heart attack, they became much closer. When Bella's mother was later diagnosed with melanoma, their bond strengthened and Bella began to spend time with the Burtons. As Sonia says, 'We were there for her.' After her mother's death in 2014, Bella and her brother Jonathan were unofficially adopted by the Burton family. Sonia is now mother to six children. She believes that helping others is food for the soul; the children are better at sharing and empathy. Sonia greatly appreciates the help and guidance from Relationships Australia[1] and CanTeen.[2]

The Burton–Gaudiosi family
Back row: Bella and Jonathan Gaudiosi, Tamika Burton;
middle row: Sam, Max; front row: Zachary, Sonia
Photo: Adrian Basnett

---

1 www.relationships.org.au
2 www.canteen.org.au

Bella Gaudiosi

*Both parents died when she was 12 years
old; now 'adopted' into the Burton family*

AUSTRALIA

> You can love someone so much, he thought. But you can
> never love people as much as you can miss them.

> John Green, *An Abundance of Katherines*

When my mother died, everything changed: there was a
new house, a new mother and new rules. Closing one door
means the opening of a new one.

What I have learned is that although it might be hard
to balance your emotions in life, I know I am the only one
who can really do that. For me, and others in this situation,
people can guess or relate to what it is like but nobody can
tell you how *you* feel.

There are times when I feel sad but also times when it
feels OK to have moved on and to have some fun. I still miss
my mum, and this quote by John Green sums up how I feel:
I miss my mother more than I thought.

Tamika Burton

Her father died when she was ten years old

AUSTRALIA

Life is a rollercoaster. It has its ups and downs. It's your choice to scream or just enjoy the ride.

Anon

I try to be positive about life but sometimes it's hard. Nothing is going to change that Dad has gone; I just have to live with this. When times are bleak, I sit outside; at other times I do want to scream and let it out. But there are times when I go with the flow and enjoy the ride. My mum is very loving and I know I have a good life. There are many others in this world who live in much worse situations than me.

There are seven of us now living together as one big family. Sometimes it is crazy but mostly I like it. I can always find a space outside to have 'time out'.

Amit Dasgupta

Former diplomat; author and photographer
INDIA

My father was a wonderful storyteller. 'The very best', my mother always said! On the last occasion that I heard him tell a story, it was to my daughter, Diya, way back in 1993, in New Delhi, India. The friendship between the two of them had always fascinated me. He was 73 years old and she was a little over five. Both of them were sitting outside, looking at the sky and talking about the stars and the night. I nursed my scotch silently, listening to them. My daughter was asking multiple questions, the ever-indulgent grandfather was patiently responding. Somehow they started talking about death and learning to let go.

'What is a star, Dadu [grandfather]?' my daughter asked. My father thought for a while and quietly whispered, 'When we die, we all become stars.' He let this sink in and then continued, 'but only when we recognize that letting go of someone we love, does not mean that we ever forget them. If we are unable to let them go, or if we continue to cling on to them when it is time for them to leave, the sky would be denied a star.' My daughter nodded and I am sure she must have understood. I didn't. Later that evening, Baba [father] and I sat down to have a drink together. I asked him how the conversation had suddenly moved from stars to death and to letting go. 'One thing always leads to another,' he said with a twinkle in his eye, 'and that is what life is all about!'

My relationship with my father is something I have always cherished. His stories fascinated me and I loved being with him. He told me once, 'Talk with everyone, listen to everyone because everyone has something to say and often, it is new and you will learn something different.'

He once took me to Mother Teresa's Nirmal Hridaya [the Compassionate Heart] in Kolkata [formerly Calcutta]. I was around 14 years old. I joined him in spending time with the dying, talking with them, cleaning their wounds and feeding them. Mother came in silently and spoke briefly with Baba and then went on to meet the inmates of the Home. I remember she held my hands and though she was frail and small in stature, her eyes were laughing and she filled the room with her presence. 'Love,' she told me when we were leaving, 'fill your heart with it for without it, life has no purpose.' I have loved and respected Mother ever since that single experience. I was not Catholic, nor were my parents, but that hardly mattered. Like many, I saw that what Mother stood for was much higher than mere religious beliefs. It was the essence of humanity.

You might be wondering what happened after the 'star story'? Well, one hot and humid night in New Delhi, cradled in my arms, my father died. My five-year-old daughter took it extremely well. I knew, then, that she had learnt to let go. When I talked to her about my father and about death, she simply said that her Dadu had become a star. In my case, it took a very long time. I struggled because I was simply unable to understand his not being there when I longed so much to simply chat with him, to argue, to seek his advice or to just walk with him and watch the sun set.

Much, much later, I saw a story in that conversation about the night and the stars and the storytelling, the love and the caring and the friendship between my daughter and my father. This led me to write *The Lost Fragrance* and later, *Lessons from Ruslana: In Search of Transformative Thinking*, mainly for my family and myself and yet it seemed to speak to many. For me, the journey of letting go had begun. One thing had led to another, and as my father always said, that is what life is all about.

Amit Dasgupta, *Once upon a Star*

This story about stars has always held a personal significance, ever since I heard my father first mention it to my daughter. It seemed like such a wonderful way of understanding and accepting death. Many years later, after my parents had both died, I was able to come to terms with their passing and to understand that 'letting go' was possible only when we accept the inevitability of death and, more importantly, when we see it as an integral part of life.

At that moment of profound grief, we are desperately in need of emotional strength, and that is why what my father said to my daughter touched my heart. Even today, I often look at the sky and the stars and say a quiet 'Thank you' to my mother and to my father, simply because I had the privilege of having them as my parents. When I see a couple of stars near one another, I am certain they must be my parents and I look forward, some day, to being the third star.

Death happens. If we are able to accept the inevitability of death, we would be able to see death with a sense of equanimity. We would then learn how we might live our life with dignity, with compassion, and with a commitment to the core values that we subscribe to. Only then would life and death have meaning.

* * *

Amit Dasgupta was formerly an Indian diplomat. After retirement he became a full-time writer. His books include *Lessons from Ruslana*, which is about recognising that death and life are part of a continuum, and *The Lost Fragrance*, which explored how understanding death allows us to let go of departed loved ones. Amit now heads a global business school in Mumbai.

Erica Stewart

Bereavement Support Services Manager, Sands
(stillbirth and neonatal death charity)

UK

> Gradually the space between the pain will get longer and
> the death of a baby becomes woven as one vivid strand
> in the whole texture of life.
>
> Sheila Kitzinger, *Women's Experience of Sex*

Over 30 years ago, I suffered the death of Baby Shane, who
died aged eight weeks.

When parents suffer the death of their baby – before,
during or shortly after the birth – the effect is traumatic and
devastating. Their world is turned completely upside down.
The process of becoming parents, again or for the first time,
which started with pregnancy, is totally derailed. Parents
find that now they have to make decisions they never
thought they would ever have to make.

Both fathers and mothers are profoundly affected by the
death of their baby. Leaving hospital without their baby is
one of the hardest things bereaved parents will ever do. They
are catapulted from joyous expectations to absolute isolation
and despair. Alongside the loss of a dreamed-of future is the
loss of self-esteem and self-image. It is the start of a very
long journey, navigating their way through grief and deep
sadness. A father's grief is not to be underestimated or
ignored as often the focus is on the mother.

I have 20 years' experience working with bereaved
parents and families and am now the Bereavement Support
Services Manager for Sands UK. My job involves supporting

parents whose baby has died. A typical Facebook message to our service might read: 'We have just found out our baby has died and that my wife has to give birth to our dead son. Please help.'

Immediately after a baby has died, it is very important that the parents have the choice to spend time with him or her; it is an opportunity that most parents welcome. Some parents take their baby home before the funeral. Others will prefer to spend time with their baby in the hospital. They can arrange to have photos with their baby, have hand and footprints taken and keep a lock of hair. Many parents have a memory box in which to keep objects and items associated with their baby, which they can add to and treasure for life.

Some may find it hard to relate to the death of a baby. They might ask, 'How can you grieve for someone you didn't know?' Although few people will have met their baby, the parents need the existence and death of their baby to be acknowledged. Usually, they welcome the opportunity to talk about their baby. They need permission to grieve and to have their expression of their grief accepted. They need family and friends around them who are not going to shy away from them if they mention their baby's name or shed a tear. Bereaved parents appreciate signs of care when people remember their baby's name, or send a text or a card on the anniversary of their baby's death. It's a huge comfort to know that friends and family have not forgotten their baby even after years. Knowing that family and friends would have enjoyed getting to know their baby, and watching her or him grow up, is a positive and helpful experience for the parents.

Feelings and reactions come in no predictable order. Grief comes in waves rather than stages, but as time goes on, the waves do get further apart and smoother. Yet there will always be unexpected triggers of grief – a song, a smell, a season, recalling approaching anniversaries, seeing pregnant women and babies with their parents.

For some, the experience of bereavement can be a time of personal growth. Sheila Kitzinger's quote may resonate strongly as grief for the baby becomes woven into the very fabric of your life. The thread of grief is always there. You have lost your child as well as part of you. In the years after Baby Shane's death, I feel that I have gradually allowed myself to see some positives in my life. I have become much more compassionate and hopefully wiser. Baby Shane's death 32 years ago has taken me on a life journey to support other bereaved parents and to train health professionals who are involved in caring for bereaved parents and families.

For each of us, the death of our baby is a major bereavement and needs to be acknowledged as one. It was a little life, not a little loss.

* * *

Erica Stewart has four children. In 1983, her third baby, Baby Shane, died aged eight weeks following major heart surgery. Erica is a qualified counsellor and has worked at Sands (www.uk-sands.org) for 20 years, supporting parents and families after the death of their baby. She also teaches midwives and health visitors and other health professionals about grieving and the uniqueness of a baby's death.

Kinny Gardner

Director, Krazy Kat Theatre Company

UK

The gay and lesbian community lost so many young people in our early battles against the AIDS pandemic. Too many funerals of too many hopeful teenagers, too many old campaigners, too many vibrant butterflies and too many ordinary mothers; all dealing with horrors they should never have endured, and in such numbers.

And yet it seems we kept our sense of humour, of wonder and of joy in the vagaries of fortune. When my late husband, Alastair, was in hospital, dying of germ cell cancer, not of AIDS, many people visited just before he died. He initially didn't want to see anyone apart from close family, but as the illness developed and the prognosis deteriorated, the call went out…

I have tried to write, here and now, about my memories of that magnificent afternoon and evening when 39 people of all shapes, colours, ages and sexes queued up at the high-dependency unit in a hospital in Chelsea, London, to chat, laugh, cry and celebrate the fact that Alastair was still here. I have so little memory of that whirl, apart from an ever-abiding joy at having been there every single minute. So, as I am neither a writer nor a journalist, I am quoting my dear and eloquent friend Karen, who had a perfect take on it:

…it was clear that your friends had so much experience of death – deaths that happened in the richness and vigour of lives so full of love and creativity – that they had developed powerful ways of supporting the patient and their loved ones through the experience of death in hospital. It wasn't left to a vicar or a health professional. I felt you'd developed practices for managing the process to make it less dreadful, kinder.

It was almost like arriving at a party, albeit a desperately sad one. One friend seemed to be designated host, welcoming visitors and managing their access to Alastair; the walls around the bed were covered with messages of love and beautiful things from home.

People knew what was happening and were in control: the coldness of the hospital environment was kept at bay. This may have been just your and Alastair's friends, but I assumed at the time that these practices may have evolved more widely…

And I assume the same. Recognition of mortality and an insistence on sharing the comfort of the moment – these strengths bring deeper courage and firmer affirmations of love and the need for the acceptance of the inevitable. Once it is named, it can be welcomed.

As a postscript, I held up pretty well, with useful bouts of weeping and shudders. But the thing that cracked my tears and laughter wide open was when a young deaf child, in a school I was performing at, signed to me, 'Very sorry, your news. Your dead friend, where is he now?!' It turned out the whole school for deaf children had held an assembly remembering Alastair, and had collected a list of questions to ask me when I next visited with a performance. How respectful, to him, to us and to me as the survivor.

* * *

Charismatic, popular and low-maintenance, Kinny Gardner has been performing and creating for over 35 years since he did *Godspell* in the 1970s. Kinny is a soloist with the Lindsay

Kemp Company and co-founded the Krazy Kat Theatre Company (Sign Language Arts) (www.krazykattheatre.co.uk). In the process of doing all of this, he has a lot of laughs. In 2015 he was awarded the BBC Community Hero Award for his services to the arts.

Pam Masini

Tertiary in the Third Order of Franciscans; Bereavement Support Worker, Child Bereavement UK; textile artist

UK

'Human beings are God's language.'[3] That is, when we cry out to God in our anguish, he responds by sending us people.

Harold S. Kushner, *When Bad Things Happen to Good People*

When Becky, our only child, was diagnosed with aggressive breast cancer two days before her 30th birthday, our world fell apart. Finding these words in Harold Kushner's book *When Bad Things Happen to Good People* summed up my sense of being 'held' by so many wonderful friends, and made me aware of the many prayers being said for Becky in different parts of the world. Now my path seems to merge with others in an extraordinary and God-given way.

Having nursed many children who died, I was acutely conscious that 'when bad things happen to good people', families cope very differently. We took our lead from Becky, who was brave and inspirational, never the victim, and determined to survive to bring up her daughter, aged two at this time. From day one of her diagnosis, she and her husband Nathan chose to be open with everyone, so as a family this was our ethos. Her 30th birthday party was an occasion I will never forget; the sense of love was tangible,

---

3   Rabbi Menachem Mendel of Rymanov

58

not only for Becky and Nathan, but for us, her parents, too. She lived for 22 months from diagnosis to her death. How could I not be strong when she was so stoic?

When people ask the question, 'How are you doing?' I answer, 'We are grieving healthily' – through times of intense sadness, and joyful times too, as Becky would have wished. From my work at Child Bereavement UK, I have learned that what children need most from adults, at times of pre- and post-bereavement, is openness and honesty, appropriate to their developmental stage. Becky and Nathan followed this approach, answering the toughest question – 'Are you going to die Mummy?' – with the honest response delivered with love and tears.

At times of grief, children's words can be incredibly poignant. 'I'll look after you now, Daddy' were the words I heard my three-year-old granddaughter say to her father when he broke the news to her that Becky had died; heartbreaking words but so precious.

For months after Becky's death I gained consolation by dipping in and out of a book called *Good Grief, Daily Meditations* by Susan L. Schoenbeck. One helpful line says, 'I choose to gather up all the stories we share and weave a rainbow.' As I love working with textiles, these words were healing and I find comfort still in creating meaningful pieces.

Some years ago I had made a crazy patchwork for the bereaved children with whom I work. Uncertain at first about its use, I came to see it as a symbol of hope. *These torn pieces of fabric have come together to be whole and strong. So we too, who have been torn apart by tragedy, can also become whole and strong again with the resilience of the human spirit.* We use this metaphor with bereaved families with whom we work.

Detail of 'Resilience' quilt as used with bereaved
families supported by Child Bereavement UK
Photo: Rosalind Bradley

Becky was not afraid of dying but was concerned for all of us who loved her so dearly. I feel Becky's personal legacy to me is to strive and make a difference in the lives of others in whatever way God moves me. Isaiah, Chapter 64, Verse 8 reads: 'We are the clay, you are our potter...' I am happy to be moulded by God.

* * *

Pam Masini is an Anglican, a Tertiary in the Third Order of the Franciscans and a textile artist. A paediatric and children's community nurse for 30 years, Pam became a volunteer hospital chaplaincy visitor after retiring. In 2005 Pam was invited to be a Bereavement Support Worker for Child Bereavement UK, a position she still holds (www. childbereavementuk.org). Pam's only child, Becky, died of breast cancer in 2013.

Reverend Peter Pereira

Uniting Church minister and counsellor

AUSTRALIA

Peter was diagnosed with oesophageal cancer in late 2013 and wrote much during his journey of aggressive surgery and chemotherapy. Throughout this time he maintained a deep faith and was a keen observer of his own responses to his new life journey. Peter passed away in December 2014 and this piece below, written by him, was shared at his thanksgiving service.

Dear friends and colleagues

This particular reflection has a personal edge to it. It emerges from my journey with cancer, and although I am a little reluctant to share these thoughts, I do so in the belief that often the most personal experiences are the most universal. It also touches on the ultimate common experience that comes to us all, death.

When I received a diagnosis of oesophageal cancer, very unusual for my age, my life and that of my family was turned upside down overnight and I was brought face to face with my mortality. So in recent months, while undergoing treatment, I have found myself reflecting upon death.

A chaplain recently shared with me that perhaps cancer has ability to be 'the disguised teacher'. When death comes knocking, there are lessons to be learned. It is as if the closeness of death provides a new set of spectacles through which to view life.

So what has my disguised teacher taught me? To even ponder upon death is counter-cultural as we live in a culture that keeps death at a distance. Our capacity to prolong life and provide distractions for the mind mean that we can spend most of life avoiding the one definite reality of life: that we are mortal and that death will come.

In recent months I have been unable to rely on that comforting illusion of death being distant. I have learned that so much of what I value in life is only of a *temporary* nature. The life I have constructed for myself over many years is only temporary. Although my life is of value, to idolise it and to set it in concrete as some kind of monument to the universe is pointless and ultimately quite egotistical. This applies to us all. At some point we all need to go through the grief of letting go of what our egos want to cling on to as important. I confess that I am still journeying with this grief.

My journey with cancer has taught me to be more grateful. I am grateful to my family for their selfless love and support. I am grateful for the amazing support I have received from friends, colleagues and acquaintances. I have immense gratitude for the skills of the medical profession without whom there would have been no hope of my continued life in this world.

And I have been deeply thankful for my Christian faith. I have found that my faith has provided hope in the midst of times that looked hopeless. It has proved to be an opportunity to take my faith for a 'test drive'. My theology felt good in theory but now I realise that it is a deep part of my spiritual DNA and I am so thankful it is a part of my life.

In the darkest times, and there have been some, I have found it is my Christian faith that has told me that life continues to have value. We only ever have the moment and each moment can be viewed as a gift. My faith also tells me that whatever lies on the other side of death is preordained. God is present in life and death and beyond death. Though

I can at best guess at what lies on the other side, it is not something to be feared but something to be welcomed. This does not mean that I want to die; in fact, I very much want to keep on living in this life. I am beginning to think that making friends with death may allow us to live more fully.

I have also come to be more appreciative of being part of a community of faith. My family and I have been upheld by the support from the praying community both in Australia and around the world. The knowledge that we are being prayed for has been almost tangible. At times, when we have not had the emotional strength to be praying for ourselves, it's as though others have been doing the praying for us.

So where has this all brought me? Well, I am not sure that I see death as the enemy any more. Instead, I see our cultural pretence of denying death as a greater enemy. Such pretence can make it harder for us when death does come knocking. It would be more helpful if we allowed talk about death back into the hustle and bustle of everyday life rather than the current mere whispers in dark hospital corridors.

* * *

Reverend Peter Pereira was a Uniting Church minister and a masters graduate in counselling. A gifted pastor, teacher and listener, Peter was committed to enabling others to thrive and believed everyone had a story that needed to be heard. He was fascinated by the intersection of spirituality and psychology and was a prolific writer in this area.

Mitchell Willoughby

Death row inmate

USA

When you realize emptiness, there is no fear.

Lama Zopa Rinpoche

Having been on death row for over 30 years, I have had to deal with major issues of anger, self-worth and forgiveness. I can truthfully say that my Buddhist practice has transformed me from being a drug and alcohol addict to being more human. I have had to learn to accept my fate. I saw how much I had hurt so many people and I came to the realisation that no matter what I did to get here, I knew I was never going to get out of prison alive. So I had to make the best of a very bad situation.

My transformation started with reading *The Hundred Thousand Songs of Milarepa*.[4] At first I did not understand Milarepa's devotion to his guru, Marpa. How could someone be so devoted? After Venerable Robina Courtin of Liberation Prison Project[5] first visited us in 1997 and said in one of her talks, 'You have to do the work, no one else will do it for you,' it really struck home. I literally had to take my life apart and rebuild it to see who I am. I had no one left to face except myself.

Robina helped me to prepare to take the *Bodhisattva* vows, the precepts. (These vows are the foundation of the Mahayana Buddhist path; they help you to commit yourself

---

4   A guide book of devotions and teachings by the 11th-century Tibetan Buddhist poet and saint, Milarepa.

5   www.liberationprisonproject.org

to the activities and life of a *bodhisattva*, an enlightened person). During this time, I not only committed them to memory, but also practised living according to them and devoting my every action to benefiting other living beings. My practice gave me insights into how people think and react to different situations and problems.

Once I accepted this new space of being, a whole new world began to open up and I was amazed at how I missed it in the first place. My life in here is now spent helping others, even at great criticism from fellow inmates. Over the years I have made many crafts for friends and family, I have written to numerous troubled people and have helped the sick and the dying here on death row. I do not do this for praise or to be recognised for it. I do it *because I can*.

This is the way it is. I created all this mess. I don't have anyone else to blame. My practice has helped me make the best of an awful situation. That's the reality. I have to own up to it and face it daily. Once I began to do this, my anger gradually lessened, as I knew it was all up to me. My family and I are now closer. My mother's mind is more at ease. I put myself here; no one else can be blamed. The burden should not be placed on my family. I have to carry it. Only when you can really see the harm that you have done to yourself and stop blaming everyone else for all your problems can you see the avalanche of heartache that you have caused others. No one will ever know how sorry I am. It still really hurts my heart even after all these years.

And whatever awaits me in the next life, I will accept it as well. I don't fear death. As Lama Zopa Rinpoche says, 'When you realize emptiness, there is no fear.'

* * *

Mitchell Willoughby is on death row awaiting execution at Kentucky State Prison, USA. In 1983, he was sentenced to death for the murders of two people (and was given a life sentence for a third murder). After he overcame his drug and alcohol addiction, Mitchell reclaimed his life through Buddhism.

FURTHER VERSES

To be blessed in death, one must learn to live. To be blessed in life, one must learn to die.

Medieval prayer

I am not afraid of death. I know so many people there.

Amy, eight-year-old Norwegian girl

Do not judge a song by its duration
Nor by the number of its notes
Judge it by the way it touches and lifts the soul
Sometimes those unfinished are
among the most beautiful
And when something has enriched your life
And when its melody lingers on in your heart
Is it unfinished?
Or is it endless?

Anon

PART 2

Death Brings Us Wisdom

In Part 2, contributors express deep insights about death and how it affects our living. The paradox of living and dying is explored: embracing death as part of life, the continuity of life and 'making friends with death'. Death can bring a healing, an increased intimacy and, despite the inescapable sadness, a sense of awe of being present at the death of others. Themes of the quest for a meaningful life and gratitude, hope, love and forgiveness in the face of dying are voiced. In addition, the difficulties of letting go for both the dying and the bereaved are recognised.

Contributors include an Anglican minister and chaplain, a 'death talker', a former palliative care physician, a music-thanatologist and clinician, a Benedictine monk, a co-founder of the Natural Death Centre, a community funeral celebrant, a professor researching the journey of dying, a London rabbi, an Open University lecturer in end-of-life practice and the Tibetan Buddhist author of the classic text *The Tibetan Way of Living and Dying*. One passage is an excerpt from a final testament written by a Trappist monk, who was murdered in 1996.

Their sentiments include:

'As we gradually realise the mysterious finality in death, we are pushed to a more profound sense of who we are.'

'What I want to ensure is that my life has
been meaningful. That I leave behind
a legacy for future generations.'

'I knew at that moment, and have known ever since,
that the best way to die is to have a heart filled with
gratitude. To be thankful for all the love in your life,
both received and given, sets your own soul at peace...'

'Death deprives us of life but in so doing it
earnestly bids us to share intimately.'

'Our dead watch over us from inside our
hearts. We talk to them, they talk to us,
and their love and wisdom bless us.'

Josefine Speyer

Psychotherapist; death education specialist;
Co-founder, Natural Death Centre

UK

Men come and they go and they trot and they dance, and
never a word about death. All well and good. Yet when
death does come – to them, their wives, their children,
their friends – catching them unawares and unprepared,
then what storms of passion overwhelm them, what
cries, what fury, what despair! ...

To begin depriving death of its greatest advantage
over us...let us deprive death of its strangeness, let us
frequent it, let us get used to it; let us have nothing more
often in mind than death... We do not know where
death awaits us: so let us wait for it everywhere. To
practice death is to practice freedom.

Michel de Montaigne, The Complete Essays

I believe we should be making friends with death and
embracing death as part of life, as all the great religions try
to teach us. To lead a good and meaningful life, we need to
remember that we are mortal. This is my daily practice and
it helps me to appreciate all aspects of my life: my health,
family, friends, the people I work with, as well as nature,
animals and the environment. Life is so fragile and we are
all here for such a brief period of time.

I know how trauma affects people. I was born in
Germany six years after the end of the war and spent my
formative years there. Trauma silences people; it creates
isolation. People are in shock and feel numb without

necessarily knowing that this is what is happening to them. Feelings get buried to protect against pain and loss. It is a form of survival but it is not much of a life. I believe we all long to be alive before we die. Everyone wants to experience happiness. The 'trotting and dancing and never a thought about death' that de Montaigne talks about is a denial of death, an attempt to avoid pain and suffering for fear that it will be overwhelming.

To me, making friends with death means facing past trauma and loss as well as learning to recognise death in its daily and mundane appearances: the small losses, the disappointments and the failures we suffer. We hurt people and get hurt; we must not hide that we are vulnerable. We need to talk to each other with a greater degree of openness and honesty. Then, when death comes, we are ready to talk to each other and to give and receive support. This is what we need now, while we are in the midst of life.

My husband, Nicholas Albery, died in a car crash in June 2001. His best friend, Nicholas Saunders, died in the same way just three years earlier. I was shocked at our friend's death and I was even more shocked at my husband's death. My husband and I had founded the Natural Death Centre and through our work we had become experts in family-organised 'green' funerals. Working together with family and friends, we were able to create truly unique natural burials for both of them on our own woodland. These funerals were beautiful and deeply meaningful and gave us all great satisfaction. It also helped us regain a sense of power at a time when these untimely deaths left us feeling helpless.

While nothing can shield us from the pain of loss, discussing funeral wishes is one way we can take death out of the closet and make it part of a normal conversation. This is best done when everyone is well and healthy. In essence, we need to live life in a meaningful and loving way, practising good communication.

At the end of their lives, people want to feel that they are loved, that their work is done, that they can forgive themselves and others. They want to feel at peace. That is part of a 'good death'. It is also what we need to have a good life. So, in the end, making friends with death is making friends with life!

* * *

Josefine Speyer is a psychotherapist based in London with a special interest in death education. She was Co-founder of the Natural Death Centre charity (www.naturaldeath.org.uk) and the Befriending Network (www.oxbel.org.uk).

Josefine has been a supervisor at a bereavement service for many years and holds death education workshops, natural death salons and death cafés.

Jennifer Briscoe-Hough

Community project innovator;
community funeral celebrant

AUSTRALIA

I live my life in widening circles
that reach out across the world.
I may not ever complete the last one
but I give myself to it.
I circle around God, around the primordial tower.
I've been circling for thousands of years
and I still don't know: am I a falcon,
a storm, or a great song?

Rainer Maria Rilke, *Rilke's Book of*
Hours: Love Poems to God

I love these lines of Rilke's. There is so much space in them, so much wildness and freedom. The leaning into the unknown, fully alive; having faith in the mystery.

I have sat with people who are dying and I have cared for the bodies of people after they die. Being at a death is like being at a birth. We are as connected as we can be.

What is always so incredible to me is that when someone we love dies, somehow we don't die too. We keep on living. We are both connected and separate.

What I know are a few simple things and I know them in my own bones. I know that fear is limited; I know that being able to be connected to death wakes me up – it catapults me to the centre of life.

I know that being able to put my hands on the dead body of someone I love helps my body understand that they have gone – it's a cellular communication. As human beings, we know how to look after our own dead – it is our work, and if we are left to do it, we find our way.

I know that all life is sacred. I know that all death is sacred.

I was with my mother during her dying. It wasn't easy. She had to work like a steam train to die. I remember thinking she had worked so hard all her life and now she had to work hard even to die. The nurses kept saying her feet will go cold just before, but her feet never went cold; she was incandescent with life when she died.

I was with her and it was like having a hurricane blow through me. It rearranged me, which I think must be the job of this enormous life. If I am paying attention, I am rearranged over and over again. And then I can lean into life in a way that expands everything, especially my heart.

I don't know what happens after we die. I am too busy being a human being. I have a spiritual life; it is the spiritual life of a human being. It's a practice to be alive and awake, and I fail at that as much as I succeed.

These words above by Rilke release me into the mystery of this life and what is required for the living of it – the wild beauty of being a human being, with the very humbling limitation of being flesh and blood and bone. I believe:

It is ordinary and necessary life.

It is beautiful and heartbreaking life.

It is exhilarating and unbearable life.

* * *

Jennifer Briscoe-Hough is the General Manager of the NSW Port Kembla Community Project, a community organisation with a reputation for developing and implementing innovative community projects. Its many projects include Tender Funerals, a not-for-profit community funeral service (www.tenderfunerals.org). Jennifer was a past Chair of the Pathways Foundation, a Vincent Fairfax Fellow and a graduate of the School for Social Entrepreneurs.

Reverend Canon Rosie Harper

Vicar of Great Missenden; Chaplain to the
Bishop of Buckingham; General Synod member

UK

And did you get what
you wanted from this life, even so?
I did.
And what did you want?
To call myself beloved, to feel myself
beloved on the earth.

Raymond Carver, *Late Fragment*

I talk to people who are dying. It's part of my work, but also part of my humanity.

In theory, we all know we will die and therefore have plenty of opportunity to think through our mortality. When we do, there are both spiritual and practical benefits. There has been a considerable shift in social attitudes in recent years. Death is more freely discussed and as a result many people are able to make more informed and personal choices. In England we are far from being able to enable everyone to have a good death, but at least it is no longer a taboo subject.

There is, however, a special time when someone has received a terminal diagnosis and has a few weeks or months to work it all out. This is sometimes the point at which a conversation with a priest could be helpful, and it is an extraordinary privilege to sit and think and maybe pray.

Some priests deal in certainties, and some folk long for certainties. The truth is that we know so very little. I can't tell people about what happens after death. It's obvious we can't do the science, and the Bible itself is very unclear. There is poetry and fantasy, as in the book of Revelation which was written by a very old man trying to express a mystery. Apart from that, there is, as I see it, the concept that we are drawn back into the being of God and of God's love.

'Will I go to hell?' is the million-dollar question. But, except for the very few ultra-literal-minded, it isn't so much a question about the future as about the past. It's asking deep questions about the quality of their lives and in particular about their relationships. You could almost say it's the 'What's the point of life?' question.

That is why I find this passage *Late Fragment* by Raymond Carver so very helpful. Once you know you are soon to die, your possessions and even your achievements become instantly insignificant. You begin to consider the inner value of your life, and stripping everything away leaves you with this simple question: 'And did you get what you wanted from this life, even so?'

My first experience of dying was my maternal grandmother. I travelled to Switzerland to say goodbye and by the time I got there she could barely talk. All she could say was, 'Much love, so much love.' She truly knew herself 'beloved on the earth'. I knew at that moment, and have known ever since, that the best way to die is to have a heart filled with gratitude. To be thankful for all the love in your life, both received and given, sets your own soul at peace and is superbly helpful for those around you.

Not long ago I watched a film made in Portland, Oregon (USA), which followed two people in their journey towards assisted dying. For both of them, in the final moments after they had taken the drugs, all they wanted to say was 'Thank you, thank you for loving me and letting me love you.'

As a priest, this little poem is probably all I want to say about God and faith.

* * *

Canon Rosie Harper was a professional singer before studying for an MA in Philosophy and Religion. Currently Vicar of Great Missenden and Chaplain to the Bishop of Buckingham, Rosie is chair of the Oxford Nandyal Education Foundation (www.indiangapyearsnandyal.blogspot.com.au) and a member of General Synod, and writes regularly for *The Guardian* and religious journals. She is deeply committed to working for issues of justice and equality.

Molly Carlile AM

Deathtalker®; palliative care activist
AUSTRALIA

When the Present has latched its postern
behind my tremulous stay,
And the May month flaps its glad green leaves like wings,
Delicate-filmed as new-spun silk, will the neighbours say,
'He was a man who used to notice such things'?

If it be in the dusk when, like an eyelid's soundless blink,
The dewfall-hawk comes crossing the shades to alight
Upon the wind-warped upland thorn, a gazer may think,
'To him this must have been a familiar sight.'

If I pass during some nocturnal blackness, mothy and warm,
When the hedgehog travels furtively over the lawn,
One may say, 'He strove that such innocent
creatures should come to no harm,
But he could do little for them; and now he is gone.'

If, when hearing that I have been stilled
at last, they stand at the door,
Watching the full-starred heavens that winter sees,
Will this thought rise on those who
will meet my face no more,
'He was one who had an eye for such mysteries'?

And will any say when my bell of
quittance is heard in the gloom,
And a crossing breeze cuts a pause in its outrollings,
Till they rise again, as they were a new bell's boom,
'He hears it not now, but used to notice such things'?

Thomas Hardy, *Afterwards*

I have spent the bulk of my career working with dying and grieving people, teaching others how to sit in personal discomfort in order to support them. Through this, I have an enormous collection of stories, poetry and songs that relate to mortality and the meaning of life. I believe that the arts provide a vehicle for people to speak the 'unspeakable' and express the 'inexpressible'.

Literary arts in particular give people an opportunity to use the words of others or metaphor to tell their own personal stories about death, grief and loss, when they may not feel comfortable using their own words. My Uncle Robbie introduced me to Thomas Hardy as a first-year university student, when he was my English Literature teacher. I discovered *Afterwards* years later and I've treasured it as it has personal resonance for me. What is it that people will remember about me after I've died? What is the legacy I will leave? What will I miss about the world of my life experience? I read it to my uncle earlier this year, hours before he died, and again at his funeral. It is a poem that links us still. Master and pupil.

Despite the obvious 'Englishness' of Hardy's work, the pictures he paints with words have both a comforting and empowering effect when I read them. This poem 'holds' me. Although some consider it melancholy, I find it affirming. I *want* people to miss me when I've died. I *want* the people I love to see something beautiful and think of me. I *want* to be embedded in the environment that continues beyond my life in a way that leaves a lasting presence.

I am not scared of death; I have been surrounded by it my whole adult life. What I want to ensure is that my life has been meaningful. That I leave behind a legacy for future generations. That somehow the years I have spent in this earthly existence have had a purpose. For me, that purpose is to change community attitudes to death and grief.

To improve death literacy so that dying and grieving people get the validation and support they so often do without. If I can change that, I will be happy.

Of course, from a purely personal perspective, I want the people I love to think of me often and with fondness. Maybe they might say, '*She* was one who had an eye for such mysteries.'

* * *

'Deathtalker'® Molly Carlile is a multi-award-winning nursing and palliative care leader and is Chief Executive Officer of South East Palliative Care in Victoria, Australia. Presenter, author and playwright, she is a champion for using the arts to engage people in conversations about life and death. Molly is an Ambassador for Dying to Know Day. (www.deathtalker.com)

Dr Michael Barbato OAM

Former palliative care physician; leader
of courses on death midwifery

AUSTRALIA

No matter what we often believe, dying is not an encounter with nothingness, devoid of all meaning. Without detracting from the pain of this journey through mourning and renunciation, I would like to show how the last interval before death can also be the culmination of the shaping of a human being, even as it transforms everyone else involved. There is still time for many things to live themselves out, on a different plane, more interior and more subtle, the plane of human relationships.

Even when one enters final helplessness, one can still love and feel loved, and many of the dying, in their last moments, send back a poignant message: Don't pass by life; don't pass by love. The ending of the life of someone you love can allow you to accompany that person to the very last step. How many of us grasp this opportunity? Instead of looking oncoming death squarely in the face, we behave as if it will never come. We lie to one another, we lie to ourselves, and instead of giving voice to the essential, instead of exchanging words of love, or gratitude, or forgiveness, instead of leaning on one another for support in the extraordinary 'crossing' that is the death of someone we love, pooling all the wisdom, the humour, and the love of which we're capable for the moment of actual encounter, we allow this final, essential, unique moment of life to be mired in silence and solitude.

Marie de Hennezel, *Intimate Death:*
How the Dying Teach Us How to Live

I identify strongly with Marie de Hennezel, a French psychologist and psychotherapist who has worked for many years in palliative care. She invites us to stop and consider our relationship with death – our perception of it, our willingness to acknowledge it, and the emotions we harbour when in its presence. She asks: Are we overwhelmed to the point of paralysis? Can we journey with death and dying? Are we capable of taking in the total landscape? Can we respond appropriately or do we hide, acknowledging neither the grief we feel nor the extraordinary gifts that present themselves at such a profound moment in time?

Her words speak to me of the enormous sadness that accompanies death and the transformative potential of love. Despite the inescapable sadness, death and dying confer upon us all a remarkable opportunity for change. The intimate dialogue that she alludes to creates opportunities for spiritual awakening and this becomes the source of healing for carers as well as the cared-for.

Marie de Hennezel challenges us to be fully present to the death of others. For in the depth of our sadness, we too may unearth an inner peace and a sense of awe that arises from the experience of redemptive love – this is the healing potential of death. Death deprives us of life but in so doing it earnestly bids us to share intimately.

The lessons to be learned from death not only guide me in my work as a palliative care physician but also in the way I lead my life and prepare for my own death.

* * *

Dr Michael Barbato's involvement with palliative care commenced in 1989. He retired in 2012 and now runs courses for professional groups and the general community on 'midwifing' death. His particular interests and current research include end-of-life care and the experience of dying. He is the author of three books on death and dying. (www.caringforthedying.com.au)

Professor Allan Kellehear

Author; medical and public health sociologist; Professor of End of Life Care, University of Bradford

UK

...the light shines in the darkness, and the darkness did not comprehend it.

John 1:5

I have been researching the journey of dying for over 30 years now – in cancer wards and hospices as well as in libraries. I have dedicated half my life to listening, observing and reading about this final experience, from people with cancer or dementia or from people on death row and death camps, or from people on doomed ships and planes or deserted islands. I have also studied death and dying in the Stone Age to the present, and in the present across different cultures and religions. People always seem a little surprised, even shocked, to learn about my line of work and they always suggest to me that it must be a rather dark or depressing line of enquiry. But it isn't, and never has been.

When I interview people with cancer with only days or hours to live, I am always impressed by how frequently suffering and pain is intertwined with personal insight, increased intimacy and the inexplicable entry of a timeless quality of enjoyment and revelling in one's social and physical surroundings. I'm always equally impressed at how this more positive and life-enhancing dimension of dying is commonly overlooked and under-described by the academic and clinical literature. At the same time, this leads me to reflect on how divergent are the survivors' and onlookers' views about the dying process when compared with the views of people actually undergoing the dying process. Onlookers always seem to see the darkness and seldom the light at the end of life. That lack of balance is not borne out by the international and historical investigations about the dying experience, nor the first-person interview-based accounts of this experience.

When I turned my attention to the last minutes of dying, I was impressed by just how many people displayed a depth of life even here, so close to death. Instead of 'nothing' or 'unconsciousness' or disturbing and disorientating hallucinations, I often found a significant prevalence of positive self-reports of comforting experiences and visions that displayed remarkable clarity and a surprising but comforting array of social relations with unseen beings. The description of these experiences – and there are thousands of well-documented cases worldwide – is often accompanied by a set of hurried scientific explanations. The lack of academic humility in these often dismissive explanations is commonly eclipsed only by their parallel lack of plausibility and precision.

Recently, I reviewed the literature on the determination of death, examining how 'brain death' was defined and linked to our general understanding of when and how death should be pronounced. Even here, in this field, where most people would expect to find no life, a disturbing abundance of evidence of the enduring presence of life boldly reveals itself. We see this in cases of pregnant women who are defined as 'brain dead' but carry their babies safely to full term nonetheless. In other cases we see the limitations of our best technologies in failing to detect life in our brains even when it is later revealed life yet remains. In these intriguing cases, when brain activity is assessed to have ceased, recovered patients report remarkable experiences and thoughts during that time. In these and many other dimensions of my work, strangely and curiously, often inexplicably, there is *persistently* light in the darkness that even darkness cannot comprehend.

For me, and for each one of us, this quote in the context of the shadow of death demands humility – preventing the door of scientific enquiry from closing against human hope and possibility. My research experiences forcibly suggest the indomitable nature of life itself, in our personal experiences, in all our different medical and historical circumstances, and inside each and every one of our biological cells, even into the darkest reaches of death itself.

∗ ∗ ∗

Allan Kellehear is a medical and public health sociologist, and 50th Anniversary Professor (End of Life Care) at the University of Bradford in the UK. He is the author of *A Social History of Dying, The Inner Life of the Dying Person* and the editor of *The Study of Dying: From Autonomy to Transformation*. (www.bradford.ac.uk/health/our-staff/professoriat/allan-kellehear.php)

Rabbi Jonathan Wittenberg

Rabbi of the New North London Synagogue;
Senior Rabbi, Masorti Judaism

UK

The dust returns to the earth as it was, and the spirit returns to God who gave it.

Ecclesiastes 12:7

And now, my dear children…I wish you – be happy, be brave. We gave you love, we gave you the foundations of life, we wanted to give you so much more… Remember your home and us, but do not grieve. Your whole life lies before you, life which you shall build at the side of your husbands. I give my blessings to them and to your children; I shall be watching over you from Heaven, and praying for your happiness.

Vera Gissing, Pearls of Childhood

Perhaps it is when we lose someone we love that we most often ask: 'What happens after death? Where is she now?'

The body reverts to earth and we become vital again in the grass, the wild flowers and the trees. Life is slowly redistributed to nourish other life.

But what happens to the spirit? I like to think that it rejoins God, like a water-drop drawn into the great river. At the same time, we both find ourselves most fully because God is the essence and energy of all being, yet lose ourselves most completely. For where now is the 'me' I used to call myself? Do personality and memory survive our dying? I only know that I don't know.

However, I am certain that the love survives, the love we share and the love we nurture in people's hearts amidst life's wonder. It grows there into blessings of future giving; it travels onwards to generations we will never know.

Our dead watch over us from inside our hearts. We talk to them, they talk to us, and their love and wisdom bless us.

* * *

Rabbi Jonathan Wittenberg is Rabbi of the New North London Synagogue and Senior Rabbi of Masorti Judaism UK. Jonathan was closely involved in the North London Hospice for many years. He has a strong interest in literature, pastoral care and Jewish spiritual traditions.

Laurence Freeman OSB

Benedictine monk; Director, World Community for Christian Meditation

UK

Live every day with death constantly before your eyes.

St Benedict, *Rule 47*

Birth and death are sacred moments in our life when our awareness of the presence of God is heightened. Like a swing door, they frame the mystery of the human journey. At the moment of birth, we enter into a journey where death is a visible and an inevitable destination. At the other end of life, the swing door of death takes us into eternal life.

As we gradually realise the mysterious finality in death, we are pushed to a more profound sense of who we are. Our identity is redefined. John Main[1] taught that when we meditate in the Christian tradition, we are entering into the dying and rising of Christ. There the ego is no longer controlling us by its clinging to our sense of self and to our desire to be in control of life and death.

Meditation is simple but not easy, because what we are doing in this practice is, in some sense, dying from moment to moment. Through our experience of meditation, we may slowly gain the courage to accept our dying and to leave our self behind.

We see death as neither failure nor enemy, but rather as part of life. Indeed, an inevitable part of our expansion of life in the resurrection of Christ. Daily meditation helps

---

1 John Main OSB (1926–1982) played a major role in the contemporary renewal of the contemplative tradition.

us to prepare for this reality and can gradually erode our excessive fear of death.

St Benedict said to his monks, 'Live every day with death constantly before your eyes.' Recognising this enhances the way we live – to live fully and therefore with joy. Slowly, we understand that we live and move and have our being – each moment, living and dying – in the ocean of God.

* * *

Laurence Freeman OSB is a Benedictine monk and the spiritual guide and Director of the World Community for Christian Meditation, a contemporary, contemplative community (www.wccm.org). Active in inter-religious dialogue with leaders of other faiths, Laurence also encourages the teaching of Christian meditation to children and students and the recovery of the contemplative wisdom in the Church and in society at large.

Carol Komaromy

Senior Lecturer in Health Studies and honorary Research Associate, Open University

UK

> We shall not cease from exploration
> And the end of all our exploring
> Will be to arrive where we started
> And know the place for the first time.
>
> T.S. Eliot, *'Little Gidding'*,
> *Four Quartets*

I spoke these words at my dad's funeral. They seemed to sum up what had happened in sharing the experience of his illness and his death. My dad was a farm boy who grew up in rural Ireland in the 1920s and 1930s. He joined the Air Force when he was 18 years old and was involved in the D-Day landings of the Second World War. He was haunted by many wartime memories and, when diagnosed with terminal cancer aged 68, he was not only facing his own death but was tormented by visions from Belsen and other war-related deaths. He needed to make sense of a world in which such inhumanity could happen. He didn't want to die, but he faced his death with courage and in the end he turned to his notion of God for comfort about what might follow.

I was a 16-year-old cadet nurse when I witnessed my first death. I was working on a medical ward and the older woman who died was someone who was acutely ill but whose death was sudden. My outstanding memory is of staring at her body for a long time, not really able to take it in – this was death. My thought was 'Oh, she's gone!' I had no idea where to, but I knew that her essence had left her body.

Since then, I have been present at the moment when many people let go of life. I have outstanding memories of being a student nurse and caring for a young man of my own age who died from bowel cancer and with whom I joked and laughed. I remember how unjust his death felt, as if there should be some sort of fairness attached to who lives and who dies.

Sometimes the deaths I witnessed were very gradual. The dying person's last breath was almost imperceptible and sometimes, as it was with my dad, more of a struggle. He noisily ground his teeth, let go of my hand and died. As an observer at the end of life, it is very hard to accept the stillness of the dead body, the lack of respiration and heartbeat.

Early in my nursing career I knew that caring for people at their end of life was to me the most important part of nursing. This was the 1970s and I became involved in the hospice movement, which was slowly establishing itself. Trying to change ideas and practice as a health practitioner was not easy, so I decided to change my career to one of research and teaching. I hope that I have made some difference.

More recently, receiving a diagnosis of grade 3 cancer and undergoing surgery, chemotherapy and radiotherapy, as well as having a stroke at the end of treatment, meant that I experienced healthcare from the patient's perspective. What got me through the hell of those treatments was the love and kindness of friends, family and colleagues, and moments of humour. Although some people in healthcare showed compassion, some were distant and others were unthinkingly cold.

I had moments when my life was in danger and I realised that death is *not* the worst thing that could happen to me. I had always imagined that I was using closeness to death and dying as a way of managing my own existential terror of nothingness. Through my sickness, I now fully realise that death *will* happen to me and it might not be so terrifying. Of course, the feeling of fatigue that went with treatment and which followed the stroke played a large part in this lack of terror.

I remember a young woman I nursed saying that she was so fatigued that she was ready to die. Indeed, my sister, who died aged 52 of a horrid degenerative disease, told me that, even though she did not want to leave her children, she was ready to die. Not everyone I have met near their end of life has been ready to die. Many people, regardless of their age and physical state, have wanted to carry on living. I can record just as many anecdotes about people extending their lives beyond the predicted end as I can about people who died 'untimely' deaths, both in the sense of being unexpected and in wanting to survive.

My research and experience have taught me that it is not easy to predict how one will feel and think when faced with the end of life. The balance of leaving a life of poor quality and facing what might come next is part of the challenge when death is anticipated. At the end of a long career and from personal experience, I believe that compassion is the most important quality when caring for people at the end of life. Compassion in being able to see people's fear and pain and wanting to do something to relieve that suffering.

For me, this quote by T.S. Eliot conveys the wisdom of life: how many of us search for meaning and find that it is really quite simple and in front of us all the time. Part of our work at the end of life is to make sense of the exploration and see it from a new perspective. This is what coming to terms with death means to me.

* * *

Carol Komaromy has been involved in end-of-life care as a practitioner, researcher and teacher since the early 1970s. She has a sustained commitment to changing practice in end-of-life care and has drawn on professional personal experiences of death and to dying to substantiate her work. Carol is a Senior Lecturer in Health Studies at the Open University, UK.

Dom Christian de Chergé OCSO

French Trappist monk, murdered in Algeria in 1996

Dom Christian de Chergé was one of seven Trappist monks kidnapped during the Algerian Civil War in March 1996. Dom Christian left instructions with his family for his spiritual testament 'to be opened in the event of my death'. Composed during December 1993 and completed on 1 January 1994, this last testament was opened on Pentecost Sunday 1996 shortly after Dom Christian and six others in his Trappist community were murdered. Their story was the inspiration for the film *Of Gods and Men*. The following is an excerpt from Dom Christian's final testament.

December 1993

If the day comes and it could be today that I am a victim of the terrorism that seems to be engulfing all foreigners living in Algeria, I would like my community, my Church, and my family to remember that I have dedicated my life to God and Algeria...

My life is not worth more than any other – not less, not more... I have lived long enough to know that I, too, am an accomplice of the evil that seems to prevail in the world around. If the moment comes, I would hope to have the presence of mind, and the time, to ask for God's pardon and for that of my fellowman, and, at the same time, to pardon in all sincerity, he who would attack me.

I would not welcome such a death. It is important for me to say this. I do not see how I could rejoice when these people whom I love will be accused, indiscriminately, of my death...

I give thanks to God for this life, completely mine yet completely theirs, too, to God. ... And to you, too, my friend of the last moment, who will not know what you are doing. Yes, for you, too, I wish this thank-you, this 'Adieu' whose image is in you also, that we may meet in heaven, like happy thieves, if it pleases God, our common Father. Amen! Insha Allah!

John W. Kiser, The Monks of Tibhirine:
Faith, Love, and Terror in Algeria

Sogyal Rinpoche

Tibet Buddhist teacher and author;
Spiritual Director of Rigpa

FRANCE/TIBET

The Western poet Rainer Maria Rilke has said that our deepest fears are like dragons guarding our deepest treasure. The fear that impermanence awakens in us, that nothing is real and nothing lasts, is, we come to discover, our greatest friend because it drives us to ask: If everything dies and changes, then what is really true? Is there something behind the appearances, something boundless and infinitely spacious, something in which the dance of change and impermanence takes place? Is there something in fact we can depend on, that does survive what we call death?

Allowing these questions to occupy us urgently, and reflecting on them, we slowly find ourselves making a profound shift in the way we view everything. With continued contemplation and practice in letting go, we come to uncover in ourselves 'something' we cannot name or describe or conceptualize, 'something' that we begin to realize lies behind all the changes and deaths of the world. The narrow desires and distractions to which our obsessive grasping onto permanence has condemned us begin to dissolve and fall away.

As this happens we catch repeated and glowing glimpses of the vast implications behind the truth of impermanence. It is as if all our lives we have been flying in an airplane through dark clouds and turbulence, when suddenly the plane soars above these into the clear, boundless sky. Inspired and exhilarated by this emergence into a new dimension of freedom, we come to uncover a depth of peace, joy, and confidence in ourselves that fills us with wonder, and breeds in us gradually a certainty that there is in us 'something' that nothing destroys, that nothing alters, and that cannot die. Milarepa wrote:

> In horror of death, I took to the mountains –
> Again and again I meditated on the uncertainty of
> the hour of death,
> Capturing the fortress of the deathless unending
> nature of mind.
> Now all fear of death is over and done.

Gradually, then, we become aware in ourselves of the calm and sky-like presence of what Milarepa calls the deathless and unending nature of mind. And as this new awareness begins to become vivid and almost unbroken, there occurs what the Upanishads call 'a turning about in the seat of consciousness', a personal, utterly non-conceptual revelation of what we are, why we are here, and how we should act, which amounts in the end to nothing less than a new life, a new birth, almost, you could say, a resurrection.

What a beautiful and what a healing mystery it is that from contemplating, continually and fearlessly, the truth of change and impermanence, we come slowly to find ourselves face to face, in gratitude and joy, with the truth of the changeless, with the truth of the deathless, unending nature of mind!

Sogyal Rinpoche, *The Tibetan Book of Living and Dying*

I wrote *The Tibetan Book of Living and Dying* with the hope that it would inspire a quiet revolution in the whole way we look at death and care for the dying, and so the whole way we look at life and care for the living. At the time, death was still very much a subject that was shunned and ignored, and in the book I sought to share the wisdom of the Tibetan Buddhist tradition, and the practical ways in which its ancient teachings can help us at every stage of living and dying.

According to the Buddha, we can actually use our lives to prepare for death. We do not have to wait for the painful death of someone close to us or the shock of terminal illness to force us into looking at our lives. Nor are we condemned to go out empty-handed at death to meet the unknown. We can begin, here and now, to find meaning in our lives. We can make of every moment an opportunity to change and to prepare – wholeheartedly, precisely and with peace of mind – for death and eternity.

In the Buddhist approach, life and death are seen as one whole, where death is the beginning of another chapter of life. Death is a mirror in which the entire meaning of life is reflected.

I have chosen this passage because it expresses just how important it is for us to reflect upon and come to truly accept change and impermanence. How liberating and healing it can be when we are able to do this, particularly when we are facing moments of crisis or loss, the death of a friend or relative, or when we are approaching the end of our life. Working with changes in life helps us to develop a sense of confidence and purpose, to move towards an emotional acceptance of death, and ultimately brings us closer to understanding our true nature, the innermost nature of the mind that underlies our entire existence and is untouched by change or death.

* * *

A world-renowned Buddhist teacher from Tibet, Sogyal Rinpoche is also the author of the highly acclaimed *The Tibetan Book of Living and Dying*. He has been teaching in the West for 40 years and is the Founder and Spiritual Director of Rigpa, an international network of Buddhist centres and groups. (www.sogyalrinpoche.org)

Therese Schroeder-Sheker

*International concert and recording
artist; clinician and educator; Academic
Dean of the Chalice of Repose Project,
School of Music-Thanatology*

USA

God, without sparing us the partial deaths, nor the final death, which form an essential part of our lives, transfigures them by integrating them in a better plan – *provided we lovingly trust in him.*

...What will be the agent of that definitive transformation? Nothing else than death... God must... make room for himself, hollowing us out and emptying us if he is to finally penetrate into us... The function of death is to provide the necessary entrance into our inmost selves.

...O God, grant that I may understand that it is you...who are painfully parting the fibres of my being in order to penetrate to the very marrow of my substance and bear me away within yourself.

...Lord...may your deep brilliance light up the innermost parts of the massive obscurities in which we move.

Pierre Teilhard de Chardin, *The Divine Milieu*

Forty-some years ago, I was a young undergraduate music student, working part-time as an orderly. Many of the residents served at the facility where I worked were in their late eighties and nineties; they had outlived friends and relatives. At the time, residents were often heavily sedated and sat in wheelchairs in front of television sets that ran as if to create the sensation of 'company'. I had become uncomfortable with the ways in which I saw death occurring as a medicalised, institutionalised, corporatised, statistical event. Death didn't signal a passage or ending of a precious individual human life so much as it did a series of institutional protocols.

I had been assigned to care for one particular man who was generally combative and yet dying of emphysema. No additional medical interventions were available for him. When I walked in the room, I heard his death rattle, and understood that his lungs had burst. Unlike the other times when he would push staff away, I saw him struggling, terrified, reaching out, for, after all, he was drowning in bed. Several of my young women friends were pregnant with their first babies at the time, and the Lamaze position of a supported birth was in my consciousness. Without thinking clinically, I responded to him as a human and a musician. I got into bed and supported his emaciated frame in Lamaze position, and sang, really quietly. Singing didn't prevent death, but it did change the way he lived his remaining minutes. He died companioned, witnessed, connected, and only later did I come to understand that, through song, our two separate sets of heartbeats and breathing patterns had become synchronised as he made his *transitus*. That was the beginning of music-thanatology. The rest is a forty-year history.

I have worked professionally for four decades in end-of-life palliative medical music-thanatology clinical practice. Most of the thousands of dying with whom I have walked or been involved had at least some time in which to prepare for their own *transitus*. Even so, what appears as a few lines on my resumé carries a different feeling from that which is inscribed in my heart.

I know catastrophic loss from the inside. This Guest invited me to awaken to something that usually eludes us in youth or young adulthood unless we live in a war zone. I did not mature into this terrain overnight, nor immediately find adequate words, but I inhabited and walked all the way *through* this world, not around it. I didn't attempt to avoid it or numb myself.

The Gospels, the mystical tradition and the Eucharist opened, nourished, deepened and sustained me then and now. Simply put: I have never had the impression that death is a single bio-medical event that occurs one-dimensionally at the last moment of an individual human biography. My sense of things is that if one is living, risking, loving and growing, then two paradoxes are fully operational: *dying is exponentially intensified living*, and *dying and becoming* are a single, mysterious and holy continuum.

In recollection, I see that we die multiple times and at different levels of being during the course of a single life. Anyone who has ever suffered a broken heart or buried their child or spouse knows that massive diminishment can arrive, yet we find ourselves inexplicably here and life requires of us that we continue.

For me, the *dying and becoming* continuum is a dynamic embodiment process; it ensouls incarnation, and deepens and defines both humanity and spirituality. We can and do grieve or mourn, yet mysterious gifts can arrive in abundance. It is possible to *die awake*. I am equally struck by the degrees of intimacy and freedom that can be discovered in this path. Jesus says: 'No one takes it from me. I lay my life down of my own accord' (John 10:18). May I connect this to a traditional way of being? There is a transformative path called *metanoia* that invites us to voluntarily *die to* or *let go of* small and large things daily: non-productive bias or resentment, impatience or blaming, illusion or attachment, pride or arrogance, fear or rage. If I choose to lay them down of my own accord, cleansing occurs. Interior space opens. These smaller deaths are purifications preparing us for the larger transition, which is to come.

I learned in my own life that the vigour and depth of each letting-go process always determines the strength, breadth and quality of the rebirth. For me, 'death' is not an enemy nor an end but core to the human-making curriculum. Generative and holy, it signals the crowning completion of one unique, irreplaceable life form. It prepares us for a new life in a new form, and His *pleroma* (fullness) which is to come!

* * *

Therese Schroeder-Sheker is a harpist, singer, composer, recording artist and clinician. Therese has maintained triple careers in classical music, graduate-level education, and clinical end-of-life care. She made her Carnegie Hall debut in 1980, and later founded the palliative medical modality of music-thanatology and the Chalice of Repose Project (www.chaliceofrepose.org). Therese is a lay Benedictine and publishes frequently on several different themes.

FURTHER VERSES

Viewed as a friend, death can remind us not to put off until tomorrow the love that we can share today, the dreams we can live today and the differences that we can make today.

Stephen L. Garrett, *When Death Speaks: Listen, Learn and Love*

When you were born, you cried and the world rejoiced. Live your life, so that when you die, the world cries and you rejoice.

Chief White Elk (Oto Nation)

If there is a meaning in life at all, then there must be a meaning in suffering. Suffering is an ineradicable part of life, even as fate and death. Without suffering and death human life cannot be complete.

Viktor Frankl, *Man's Search for Meaning*

PART 3

Working Closely
with Death

How do professionals who engage with death on a daily basis cope and understand this subject? The following contributors reveal how their roles and responsibilities have influenced their thoughts and approaches to death.

They include a war artist whose painting of Afghans offers a glimmer of hope; a Brazil-based oncologist whose AIDS patients taught her how to live; a theologian who creates sacred vigils for the dying; a senior GP who is committed to treating terminal illness at home; an obstetric social worker who bears witness to parents' grief; and an ethical entrepreneur who is involved in digital legacy. An ICU chaplain values caution with words; an ICU doctor explains why he relates to Japanese death poems; a forensic anthropologist reminds us of the importance of respectful communication; and a senior coroner sees death as part of the continuum of life itself. An independent funeral celebrant gently asks us to consider how we want to be remembered, and a Canadian funeral director reflects on having respect for the deceased body.

Their sentiments include:

'...in my own late autumn I hope more
for a reinvention of dying.'

'...it is the spiritual companionship of another
that a dying person often seeks and needs.'

'To stand with people at the darkest of times, bearing
witness to the outpouring of their grief and love for
their baby, balances the burden of sadness I might bear.'

'Death is simply a part of the continuum of life itself.'

'...I believe that as the body fades, our
inner spiritual side becomes stronger.'

'The words comforted me then
and they comfort me still.'

Deborah de Wilde OAM

Obstetric social worker and former midwife

AUSTRALIA

Truly, we live with mysteries too marvellous
    to be understood.

How grass can be nourishing in the
    mouths of the lambs.
How rivers and stones are forever
    in allegiance with gravity
        while we ourselves dream of rising.
How two hands touch and the bonds will
    never be broken.
How people come, from delight or the
    scars of damage,
to the comfort of a poem.

Let me keep my distance, always, from those
    who think they have the answers.

Let me keep company always with those who say
    'Look!' and laugh in astonishment,
    and bow their heads.

Mary Oliver, *Mysteries, Yes*

Birth and death are usually two distinct events separated by many years of a life hopefully well lived. When birth and death collide, the pain, shock and confusion are devastating. How can parents make sense of this?

This is the place of my work as a social worker and former midwife: the death of a baby.

My contact with a family may begin soon after the ultrasound that confirms an unborn baby's death. At other times I may be summoned to support a family who is being transferred to theatre for the urgent delivery of their baby, or to be with a family whose newborn is gravely ill. To say that I meet parents at a time of enormous distress is an understatement. They might be sitting alone in a delivery suite, dry-eyed, silent, stunned, having just been told that their yet-to-be-born or newly born baby has died. At other times the parents' anguish is immediate and I may enter the room to the cries of the mother howling, pleading for a reprieve from the knowledge of her baby's death, begging for this truth to be reversed.

Devastating news followed by interventions and decisions. All around them, the business of the hospital and the world continues unabated.

My part in this is nothing new or revolutionary: it is what midwives and social workers and women have done since time immemorial. It is a time of bearing witness, and of holding the space to create a sense of safety and privacy and unhurriedness.

When I am with a family, I explain I will be there for them and that there will be much for us to discuss, that we will go slowly and gently and at their pace. A sense of trust develops and a space to think and feel opens up. We might talk through the process of labour or caesarean section; we talk about the baby, how the baby may look and feel, the understandable fearfulness parents may feel at the thought of seeing their baby, what they feel they need to do around the baby. We talk about love and fear. We talk about love being their guide, their compass.

I am physically very present with them as people. I will hold them as they quake with emotion, I stroke their hair, I croon those mother sounds, catch their tears. I cajole them into eating and drinking, I advocate for them, negotiate for them, gently lead them to a place where their own 'knowing' of what they need to do for themselves and for their baby can unfold.

We may meet the baby together but not always. Sometimes moments, hours or days may pass before it feels right for the parents to be with the baby. Sometimes their meeting may be fleeting. For most, it will take place over a number of days, and often includes other close family members and friends.

To hold your own dead child in your arms is the most intimate and stark of experiences. All the senses are engaged: the touch of the baby's skin, the silkiness of the baby's hair, the intoxicating baby smell, the weight of a small foot held in the palm of the hand – all the characteristics of the baby that mark its uniqueness, its individuality.

I see parents transformed time and again by the loveliness of their baby, even the most damaged, abnormal or tiny little baby. Amidst the distress of the baby's deadness, I see the claiming of the baby as a baby, as their baby. I watch them trace with unsteady fingers the outline and contours of their baby's face and body, committing it to memory, much deeper and more profound than any photographic image I might take.

Over time we talk about parting with the baby's body, and together we will nestle the baby in the casket in preparation for his or her burial or cremation. Some families may choose to take their baby home overnight. We plan the rituals around remembering and farewelling the baby. We may talk about the legacy of this life unlived.

As we go on talking, we talk about the why: the why of the baby's death, why them, why their little baby, why any baby. We talk about the baby having gone on without them to who knows where and what a total disruption to the natural order of life it is that this little baby should die before its parents. The knowledge that death is not reserved for the ill or the elderly strikes a brutal truth for many.

Many times, when learning of my work, people will wonder at the sadness and weightiness of such a role. How can I describe for them the power of love at such times? To stand with people at the darkest of times, bearing witness to the outpouring of their grief and love for their baby, balances the burden of sadness I might bear.

It is about the mystery of life, and of death in life. It is about the power of love and the ties that bind and endure. It is about the love and vulnerability that parents all over the world and all over time feel for their children. It is what makes us human.

* * *

Deborah de Wilde is a Sydney-based obstetric social worker. She was awarded the Order of Australia Medal (OAM) in 2005 in recognition of her support to bereaved parents. Deb was an early exponent of documenting the lives of these babies through photography, and pioneered the approach where parents are offered the opportunity to see, hold and spend time with their stillborn or dying baby. (www. stillbirthfoundation.org.au)

Diane Roche

Intensive Care Unit Chaplain,
Royal North Shore Hospital
AUSTRALIA

May the gentleness of the water
soften the tensions within us.
May the wisdom of the earth
open us to mystery.
May the simplicity of air
capture our hearts.
May the flame of the Spirit
give us hope, courage
and strength
as we continue on our pilgrim way.

Celtic Blessing

In times of grief, we often hear the expression 'words are inadequate' to convey sorrow, sympathy or comfort to a bereaved family member or friend. In fact, words can sometimes be intrusive and actually hinder helping the bereaved.

In the intensive care unit (ICU) where I work, I am in the presence of dying and death each day. Very early on, I learned to be cautious with words and usually I say very little to the family of the dying patient during their bedside vigil. Instead, I do what I can, along with the nurse, to enable the patient and family to have as much privacy and intimacy as possible, in the midst of the often frenetic and noisy activity of the acute clinical environment.

Then there are those times when words are just right. The author of Ecclesiastes Chapter 3 – 'To every thing there is a season' – left us with the timeless advice: 'A time to be silent and a time to speak.'

Not long ago in my own moment of intense, almost destabilising grief, I experienced profound comfort and stability from the words of this Celtic blessing. My younger brother, Damian, had died very suddenly and we, his family, still in the haze of shock and disbelief, stood together as his Requiem Mass was concluding. The priest then turned towards us and spoke this beautiful Celtic blessing. The words comforted me then and they comfort me still.

* * *

Diane Roche has been Chaplain to the Intensive Care Unit of the Royal North Shore Hospital in Sydney for the past 18 years. The unit provides treatment and care for patients who are suffering life-threatening illnesses and critical injuries from Sydney and New South Wales. As part of the multi-disciplinary team, Di's role is to offer spiritual and emotional support to the patients, their families and to the staff.

Arabella Dorman

War artist and portrait artist

UK

Taqalla Baraye Zenda Mandan (Struggle to Survive), 2014
Photo: Arabella Dorman

If God exists, he is like the sun, giving not only light and heat, but casting shadows.

Ancient Eastern proverb

Struggle to Survive is at once a painting about light and shadows; about life and death.

I witnessed this scene in southern Afghanistan, where a child had been brought into a sparse medical outpost by her father. With deliberate echoes of a Christian triptych, the sacrificial figure in white, held in an embrace of universal parental love, is placed in the centre. Death, bereavement and suffering surround her.

The pain of death, however, mingles with resilience and strength of spirit, written in the child's defiant face and the father's tender gesture. In painting this, I seek to illustrate not only the appalling cost of war, but also the continued love, hope and courage that rise up from its embers.

* * *

Born in 1975, Arabella Dorman has gained an international reputation as a portrait painter and as a war artist. Arabella has painted portrait commissions for many prominent figures and establishments in Britain, and her work hangs in public institutions and private collections around the world. Arabella's military paintings are drawn from first-hand experience of working with British forces in Iraq and Afghanistan. (www.arabelladorman.com)

Dr Megory Anderson

Anglican theologian and author;
Founder, Sacred Dying Foundation
USA

Do not fear, for I am with you,
do not be afraid, for I am your God;
I will strengthen you, I will help you...
I have taken you by the hand and kept you.

Isaiah 41:10, 42:6

In my Anglican tradition, God is not only transcendent – outside of us – but also immanently alongside of, and within, each of us. In the Christian New Testament, we know God through the Incarnate Jesus: God-with-us. We see how God is with us in the words of the Hebrew prophet Isaiah: 'For I, the Lord your God, hold your right hand; do not fear, I will help you.' Jesus confirms this when he tells his disciples not to be afraid. He is with us, even until the end.

Except...we can't really see God, nor touch God, nor feel God's hand in ours. And when it is time to face our dying, we *are* fearful. That is why I sit with the person who is dying.

I sit vigil – that is my calling – and, time and again, a simple request comes in the form of touch. 'Please just hold my hand. Don't leave me.' I can do that because I am part of what St Paul calls the Body of Christ. I can be 'someone with skin on' in the here and now for those who need to feel God's hand in theirs.

Sitting vigil – being present, waiting, holding – is central in caring for those at end of life. I create sacred space, setting apart the ordinary, cluttered space around the bed, making it clean and ready to hold the experience of dying. Many times the person is afraid, in pain, angry, confused. Tools such as music, books, candles, personal photographs or mementoes, all help the person feel protected in the journey to death. These are the material, earthly things that can create solace.

More importantly, it is the spiritual companionship of another that a dying person often seeks and needs. If we can be present for each other during moments of fear and aloneness, especially at the sacred time of death, then we can make God real for each other.

But what happens when the person dying cannot find God at all? I have learned throughout the years to ask about love.

'Who have you loved in this life? Can you close your eyes and feel love inside your body? Where does it live?'

Most often the answer is 'Right here, in my heart.'

I smile, and I place my hand over that person's heart.

'Then that is where God lives. Always. Try to stay in that place of love, and you will be fine.'

As much as my faith speaks of God's love, even through darkness, I can't always know it is felt by the person in my care. What I can know is that my hand can be there to hold another's, bringing comfort, love and the assurance of God's promise: 'I hold you by the hand. Do not be afraid.' That is the blessing of a sacred dying.

* * *

Megory Anderson is an Anglican theologian, author and Founder of the Sacred Dying Foundation, based in San Francisco (www.sacreddying.org). She has lived in a monastic order, studied comparative religions and, in 2012, completed her PhD research in the theology of the dying from Canterbury Christ Church, UK. For the past two decades, Megory has been providing end-of-life spiritual counsel and comfort to individuals of all faiths.

Dr Peter Saul

Intensive care unit doctor,
John Hunter Hospital

AUSTRALIA

On a journey, ill:	*Tabi ni yande*
my dream goes wandering	*yume wa kareno o*
over withered fields.	*kakemeguru*

Matsuo Basho

Illness lingers on and on	*Yami yamishi*
till over Basho's	*hate ya okina no*
withered field,	
the moon.	*kareno-zuki*

Gimei

Yoel Hoffman, *Japanese Death Poems*

Basho wrote this death poem (*jisei* in Japanese) four days before his death in the winter of 1694. The image of 'withered fields' was a common metaphor for winter at that time, but here it serves as the landscape of his dream – the inescapable conclusion to his life. Life itself in other death poems is often referred to as a dream, of having lived on the 'floating world' (*ukiyo*).

Gimei responds with a death poem that adds the powerful image of the late-autumn moon (*kareno-zuki*), in this context perhaps a symbol of spiritual attainment or realisation. Something beyond even death.

Jisei, or 'farewell poems to life', were generally short (*tanka*) or very short (*haiku*), written close to death and included with documents such as the will. They were sometimes provocative, even rude, but always included a subtle message to the thoughtless young of the next generation.

My work is with those struggling to live. Many die. I have witnessed thousands of unwelcomed deaths in intensive care units in several countries. Increasingly, those dying in ICU have reached their own time of withered fields, their own winter. The hope in all our hearts is of cure, or at least the extension of this life in a reduced way. But life for many seems more like illness lingering on and on.

I live in Australia – the most successful society on earth at preventing premature death, but possibly the least ready for the inevitable final failure. Few here die in the place of their choosing: most are in acute care hospitals like mine, among caring strangers like me. Few see death coming, or have had any chance to prepare. There are no famous last words. Are there dreams? Is there a late-autumn moon?

I grow older myself, and will soon celebrate 40 years as a doctor. For most of this time I hoped my legacy would be one of lives saved, deaths averted. But in my own late autumn I hope more for a reinvention of dying. I do not like the term 'good death', but I do believe that we could avoid making death worse. And the first step to a less worse death would be in acceptance.

I love *jisei* for this quality above all. Japanese death poems are rich in irony and sometimes paradox, but all start with the acceptance that death will come. They contain the most simple and profound of all gifts to those we leave behind – a tiny fragment of who we were in life.

* * *

Dr Peter Saul is an intensive care specialist with 35 years' experience in three different countries. He has been present at the deaths of 4500 people and, more importantly, in the days leading up to those deaths, in the hard decisions that had to be made to let those people go. He is concerned that the medicalisation of dying has been scary and disempowering, and is working towards an ethic of more personal responsibility. (www.theconversationproject.org)

Stephen Olson

Executive Director, Royal Oak Burial Park
CANADA

...the good work of a religious woman, that she poured out a precious ointment over His limbs, and did it for His burial: and they are with praise commemorated in the Gospel, who having received His Body from the cross did carefully and with reverend honor see it wound and laid in the sepulchre.

May the tender care for the body of our deceased, which is destined for eternal resurrection, be a manifestation of the faith and love within us.

> St Augustine, paraphrased from *The Retractions,*
> *City of God, Teachings of Church Fathers*

The body is the garden of the soul.

> Jewish Proverb

As I have pursued my career in death care, I have sought out a deeper understanding of St Augustine's meditations on death and the care of the dead. Augustine wrote at length about the meaning and importance of funeral rites and for the body to have a dignified and respectful burial. These teachings are the essence of my working philosophy and how I relate to bereaved families.

While much has changed in 40 years around how funerals are held, at the very core of each death is how much is the body respected, how does the family observe the death, and how do they incorporate that death into their lives?

In recent years, I have been troubled by the growing trend of depersonalising the body of the deceased. The commercialisation of funerals, such as unnecessary embalming, costly caskets/urns, maudlin buildings and measuring success by strong profit margins, has done a great disservice to the public's understanding of *what is the purpose of having a funeral service.*

Many people are now seeking and exploring other options to the conventional funeral. New trends, such as green burials, home funerals, death doulas (midwives) and families insisting on more active participation in the care of their dead and holding meaningful services, are changing what constitutes a funeral service today and in the future.

Since 2008, Royal Oak Burial Park has offered green burials. This means no embalming, a simple, biodegradable shroud or casket and a direct earth burial at a site dedicated to ecological restoration and conservation. For people who are mindful of the cyclical nature of life, green burial is becoming a spiritually fulfilling alternative to a conventional burial or cremation.

Wherever possible, I try to emphasise the importance of having respect for the body of the deceased, its dignified burial or cremation, and the value of some form of funeral rite – in whatever form a family chooses.

This Jewish proverb, 'The body is the garden of the soul', succinctly reminds me of the importance of our bodies in both life and in death. Having been the vessel or 'garden of the soul', our deceased body deserves the respect of having an honourable and proper farewell.

* * *

Stephen Olson, a Catholic, has worked in death care services for 40 years. He has been an embalmer, crematorium operator, funeral director and a funeral service manager. In 1997, he changed to cemetery management when he was appointed Executive Director of Royal Oak Burial Park, British Columbia, Canada. Royal Oak Burial Park was Canada's first urban green burial site (www.robp.ca).

Dr Soren Blau

Senior forensic anthropologist, Victoria
AUSTRALIA

Looking at death, I do not accept it.
Seeing death, I know it is inevitable.
Knowing of my eventual death, I accept it.
Death will happen, there is nothing to
be done, no preparation for it other
than being good while I am alive.
There is no way for me to be sure of my body
position in death, until the mortuary bends and
twists me to fit the mold of death in my coffin.
There is no way of knowing the mode – the
how – of my death until it is upon me and I
will not know of it, being dead already.
The 'why' of my death will remain always
a mystery clothed in human reasons, but
it will offer little consolation, because no
one can know the reasons 'why'.
Aspects of death are always unknown to the dead,
and beyond human explanations no one can
truly say what it is or why we even accept it.
Through all the sorrow it brings to loved one's
hearts, death cannot be accepted, yet it is.

RoseAnn V. Shawiak, *Aspects of Death*

As a forensic anthropologist, I routinely recover, examine and record the remains of deceased individuals. I 'understand' death from a scientific, intellectual perspective, but the emotional and philosophical 'why' remains, in many cases, unanswered. Shawaik's 2013 poem *Aspects of Death* aptly captures my view that although I know death is inevitable, the 'why' of so many deaths remains unanswered. I often find it emotionally difficult to accept the 'why' of death, particularly in cases where the circumstances and timing are random and have no logical explanation.

I believe that once we die there is nothing more. Consequently, for me, living a life underpinned by honest and respectful communication and continual self-reflection about how we interact with and impact on others is pivotal. As Shawiak says, 'no preparation for it other than being good while I am alive'.

I work in an environment where I am part of a team that looks after deceased individuals in a caring and respectful manner so that some aspects of the 'why' may be provided to surviving family members, friends and/or community. While I contribute to bringing dignity to those who have often died in unpleasant and violent circumstances, the information is really only meaningful and important to the living: 'aspects of death are always unknown to the dead'.

Although I am not concerned about my own death, I fear the emptiness and loneliness that the death, particularly a sudden or unexpected death, of those I love and feel connected to will bring. The world is a large place and finding and developing friendships, understanding and love takes time and investment: relationships are unique and often impossible to replace. Yet the reality is that at some point we must all face being truly alone.

* * *

Dr Soren Blau is the Senior Forensic Anthropologist at the Victorian Institute of Forensic Medicine where she undertakes domestic and international casework. She is an Adjunct Senior Lecturer in the Department of Forensic Medicine at Monash University, Founding Fellow, Faculty of Science, at the Royal College of Pathologists of Australasia and the recipient of a Churchill Fellowship. Soren also contributes to journal and book publications.

Dr Irene Adams

Oncologist and immunologist;
Founder, Clínica Ammor

BRAZIL

...though our outward man perish, yet the inward man
is renewed day by day.

2 Corinthians 4:16

As a young oncologist, I dealt with death by concentrating
on those patients who were living and doing well. For those
whose cancers were not improving and who were going to
die, I tried to emphasise the positive aspects of their current
situation and to make them more comfortable in small ways
during their final days. But I confess I also tried not to be
there at their end.

Then I met the world of AIDS, where, in 1987, the
mere diagnosis was a sentence of death. These people had
tremendous guilt, lived in isolation and had to deal with the
fact that they were going to die. It was a very, very rough
time in my life, sitting across the table from people, telling
them they had AIDS. Yet once these patients knew they
were dying, they started to live. They also taught me how to
live and freed me to realise that you can only live fully once
you accept your own death. My life was deeply enriched.

I discovered that in a profession and world where people,
especially doctors, avoid death and dying, I was able to deal
with it, and help others to deal with it. By the time I took
over a diocesan clinic for terminal cancer and AIDS patients
in Belo Horizonte in 1995, AIDS was a treatable disease.

Yet our cancer patients were exclusively declared 'beyond therapeutic reach'.

Without knowing it, this was a mission that I had been preparing for all my life. We were a multiprofessional team where everyone – from the nurses, doctors and pharmacy staff to the receptionist, cleaning and kitchen staff – carried out our mission of 'attending to the needs of our patients and their families'. A cleaning lady who had been hired shortly after I took over said, 'I never wanted to work around dying people, but here I learned that they are just the same as other people.' She and her colleagues had our full permission to put down their mops and listen to the patients, if they wanted to talk.

The fact that the staff shared my attitude towards *living in the face of death* was transmitted to our patients and their families. Families were encouraged to visit all day long and spend the night if they could. Many of our terminal cancer patients had no families, so we built a team of volunteers and trained them, one visitor to one patient to the end.

We had a monthly Mass where I had the privilege of participating in religious celebration with my colleagues, our patients and their families. The padre who founded the clinic discovered that people who knew that they were dying not only manifested the known behaviour described by Elisabeth Kübler-Ross – denial, anger, bargaining, depression and finally acceptance – but also revealed one more phase – seeking religion. The lapsed Catholics and Protestants asked to see a priest or pastor; Jews requested a rabbi.

When the above passage from Corinthians was read during a retreat, many years ago, it clarified all that I felt about death and dying, in the light of Christ's teachings. It has become my anchor phrase because I believe that as the body fades, our inner spiritual side becomes stronger. Certainly this has been my experience with my patients.

* * *

Dr Irene Adams is a medical oncologist, an immunologist specialising in AIDS, an ecumenical Christian and a widow. She studied in California and has worked in Brazil since 1976. Irene began working with AIDS patients and later with street children in Belo Horizonte. After rediscovering her faith, Irene founded Clínica AMMOR – Ação Multiprofissional com Meninos em Risco (Multiprofessional Action with Children at Risk) (www.ammor.org.br).

Dr Louise Jordan

GP and Senior Partner, Baslow Health Centre; Founding Trustee, Helen's Trust

UK

Don't cry because it's over, smile because it happened.

Attributed to Dr Seuss

As a GP of some 30 years, I am sad that so many of my colleagues, especially in a hospital setting, see death as a failure. Death is not a failure. It is inevitable for us all; sometimes it is untimely and sometimes too soon and sometimes tragic, but it is always inevitable. Our duty as physicians is to do our best to negotiate a good death for each individual and to be with them and their family on that journey.

I have become disheartened by the fact that many patients receive invasive treatments towards their final days and hours of life in hospital. Futilely offering therapies to those with advanced malignancies when the therapy itself is likely to shorten or at the least reduce the quality of life is unacceptable. Failing to recognise that death is inevitable and often imminent but still taking blood tests and treating the numbers rather than the individual is barbaric. Surrounding the dying by visiting restrictions, drips and other barriers is inhumane and undignified.

Everyone should be entitled to a good death, and those important to that individual are also entitled to a good and healthy bereavement. This is a time to grieve the passing of a loved one, but also to celebrate their life and not be fixated on unhappy memories of the last few days.

I believe passionately in the importance of communicating well and having a relationship with my patients so that I can

134

understand their wishes and concerns, and I am privileged to work in my practice with like-minded individuals. What most people truly want is to be able to die at home, and it is so sad that that is often not achieved just because no one has really thought about what would be needed to enable someone to have that choice. On the back of this frustration I co-founded a charity in 2001 called Helen's Trust to enable the terminally ill to have the choice to stay in their own home. Increasingly, we are filling the gaps of social care by providing carers and sitters. The charity is also uniquely placed to be truly responsive and imaginative, and aims to provide what is needed in each unique situation to enable someone to die in their own home.

Although the majority would prefer to die in their own home, there are some who wish to die in a hospice and this is equally valuable. I suspect few would choose to die in a busy acute hospital.

In 2011 I lost my lovely husband of some 26 years. He was a neurologist with a brain tumour – a cruel irony. I was able to care for him at home and, amidst my dreadful loss and grief, I and my family and friends took great comfort that he was able to stay and live and die at home. After his death, my youngest son, then 15 years old, was given this quote, attributed to the famous Dr Seuss, by a school friend and it gave him great comfort.

* * *

Dr Louise Jordan qualified in medicine from Nottingham University in 1985. She married in 1985 and has two sons. Louise is a senior partner at Baslow Health Centre in the Peak District, UK, and is a Founding Trustee of Helen's Trust, a local charity that enables those with terminal illness to stay in their own home (www.helenstrust.org.uk).

Su Chard

Independent funeral celebrant

UK

I lay my head to rest and in doing so
Lay at your feet the faces I have seen
The voices I have heard, the words I have spoken
The hands I have shaken, the service I have given
The joys I have shared, the sorrows revealed.
I lay them at your feet and in doing so
I lay my head to rest.

Traditional Celtic blessing

I often use these words just before the funeral service enters the time of committal. It can signpost the moment of the deceased's transcendence from physical presence to treasured memory. For many, this moment has much deeper connotations but, whatever the mourners' feelings, it is always a pivotal time in the funeral rite and needs careful thought.

Over the past couple of years, I have been trying to understand more what it is I really do. I have come to the conclusion that as well as providing a funeral service for the deceased, I am also helping the living to consider how they will remain.

I love detective stories and often wonder if I was found dead what the contents of my handbag would say about me. At the moment there is an acorn, a lipstick I regretted buying, my diary, my purse, a bottle of ink, my fountain pen, a feather, sweet wrappers, an all-singing-and-dancing penknife and photos of my husband and daughters. Do you know me yet? Oh my goodness, I hope not. There is more to all of us than first appearances.

We therefore could consider telling our stories to those we love and also documenting them for use in our funerals. As this blessing says, to truly 'lay at the feet' of our loved ones, we need to tell them what made us happy and thankful in life. If we don't do this, our family and friends may not tell our whole story when we are gone; they can only tell *their* version of it.

It is up to us to consider how we remain and to decide what we would like to include in our post-mortem narrative that will travel through the years. Jorge Luis Borges so eloquently and simply confirms this in his poem *Elegy for a Park*: 'we are living now the past we shall become'.

* * *

Su Chard, a Quaker, is an independent celebrant creating funerals that bridge the secular and religious needs of families and the deceased. She is studying at the Centre for Death and Society at the University of Bath. Su offers training and advice in creating memorials for schools coping with the death of a child or a staff member. (www. agreatwaytogo.co.uk)

James Norris

Founder, DeadSocial.org and the
Digital Legacy Association

UK

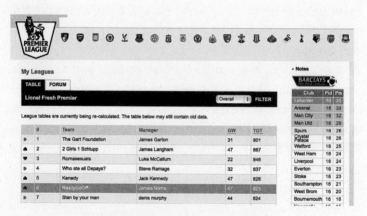

Fantasy Football League Table

Fantasy Football allows you to pick a football team each year (in the virtual world). You then receive points depending on how well your chosen players perform each week when playing in the Premiership (in the real world). This league was set up following the death of my good friend and university housemate Ben Birch who died from sudden adult death syndrome (SADS), aged 29.

Photo: James Norris

The league I play in only includes Ben's friends and helps to raise money for the charity Cardiac Risk in the Young (CRY). Ben used to play fantasy football and our mutual friend Andrew Hadley thought it a fitting idea to create a league in his honour. The name of the league changes every year but it always revolves around Ben.

This year's league is named after Ben's fictional World Wrestling Entertainment (WWE) computer game character 'Lionel Fresh'. Lionel Fresh was an exaggerated personification of Ben and designed and played with by Ben in the WWE computer game.

I chose to include the screenshot of the league and explain the context at length to highlight one example of just how intertwined our lives have become with the virtual.

Despite being in the digital realm, the league is a very personal, relevant and ongoing form of both remembrance and respect for Ben. It unites many of his friends, no matter what we are doing and where we are in the real world.

Technology and the Internet have changed the way in which many people grieve and remember their loved ones. I do not have any physical photos in London. All my photos, including those of Ben, are spread across Facebook, hard drives, mobile phones and my computers. This provides instant access to them at any given time.

I now spend my life working in a field that I call 'digital end-of-life planning'. My ongoing work includes supporting hospices, patients, charities and the National Health Service (NHS) in areas relating to digital legacy, end-of-life planning and end-of-life care.

I founded the social media organisation DeadSocial.org which provides tools and tutorials for the general public to help address death in today's connected world. Our tutorials range from 'Using iTunes playlists to decide which songs should be played at the deceased's funeral' to 'How to download your Facebook data and pass it on to your next of kin'. Our free 'goodbye and legacy tool' enables our users to create a series of private messages. These are only distributed online and to their social media accounts once they die. In doing so, each person is able to bring their digital lives to a managed ending in their own time and in their own unique way.

The Digital Legacy Association provides support, training and frameworks for healthcare professionals and those delivering end-of-life care in all areas relating to

Internet-connected devices (such as mobile phones and computers) and social media. Each year we run the Digital Legacy Conference and publish the Digital Death Report.

The Internet has been the biggest catalyst for change since the industrial revolution. If you do not use the Internet and social media sites (such as Facebook and Twitter), it may be hard to comprehend the value and comfort that they now bring to many in both life and death.

* * *

James Norris is an ethical entrepreneur who explores how technology and social media can help end-of-life care. He founded the social media organisation DeadSocial.org (www.DeadSocial.org) and the Digital Legacy Association (www.DigitalLegacyAssociation.org).

Chinyere Inyama

Senior coroner

UK

Life and death are one thread, the same line viewed from different sides.

Attributed to Lao Tzu

This quote neatly sets out my own personal beliefs around death and how they underpin my interpretation of my role as a coroner. Facing up to death and all it brings is my daily business.

I regard the coroner's role as analogous to that of a midwife. Midwives assist in managing the pain of ushering life in, and I assist in managing the pain of ushering life out. There is a period of gestation and changes to the psyche prior to birth, and similarly there is a period of bereavement and changes to the psyche after death. The birth of the person is the start of the thread and the death of the person is the end of the thread. Death is simply a part of the continuum of life itself.

* * *

Chinyere Inyama sits as the senior coroner for West London, one of the busiest coroner areas in England and Wales, having previously sat as a Mental Health Tribunal judge. Philosophically and ethically, Chinyere describes himself as an agnostic existentialist humanist.

FURTHER VERSES

Thou know'st 'tis common. All that lives must die,
Passing through nature to eternity.

William Shakespeare, *Hamlet*

Life and death are but phases of the same thing, the
reverse and obverse of the same coin... Death is as
necessary for man's growth as life itself.

Mohandes Karamchand Gandhi, *Young India*

I give you this one thought to keep –
I am with you still – I do not sleep
I am a thousand winds that blow,
I am the diamond glints on snow,
I am sunlight on ripened grain,
I am the gentle autumn rain.
When you awake in the morning's hush,
I am the swift, uplifting rush
Of quiet birds in circled flight.
I am the soft stars that shine at night.
Do not think of me as gone –
I am with you still – in each new dawn.

Native American prayer

Death and the Circle of Life

Death is part of our natural life cycle. It is not necessarily the enemy; it just is. Although the brevity of life is acknowledged, death is also a guide to living.

Part 4 presents some unique perspectives. A Buddhist cancer survivor writes about cancer survivors who re-emerge to celebrate life, while a peace activist recognises our continuity through future generations. A chief executive and an art therapist both remind us that good memories are the medicine of life and are our legacy. An Amnesty International activist writes about her campaigning against the death penalty, and an obituary writer expresses his belief in a transcendent human spirit.

For a Muslim scholar and a British Army Chaplain, death is the start of a new journey. Others have a different understanding: a clinical psychologist believes people should choose their own time of dying; an emeritus consultant psychiatrist imagines death as 'And now for something completely different'; and a mortician describes death as 'being green as the earth'.

Their sentiments include:

> 'To be prepared for the moment of death I
> would need to feel that I had lived fully.'

'...it is through our creativity that
our soul gets to speak.'

'The lives of the living are immeasurably enriched
by contemplating those who have departed.'

'I like to think that my little candle is heading into
a searchlight of brilliance beyond my dreams.'

'...death is a comma, not a full stop.'

Sughra Ahmed

*Chair, Islamic Society of Britain; Senior
Programmes Manager, Woolf Institute*

UK

Come, come, whoever you are!
Wanderer, worshipper, lover of leaving
It doesn't matter.
Ours is not a caravan of despair.
Come, even if you have broken your vow a thousand
times
Come, yet again, come, come.

Maulana Jalaluddin Rumi

This inscription on Rumi's shrine captures the essence of our journey, one part of which is life; the other is the life that will follow beyond this physical realm. Death is the closing of a chapter to a life that we have taken part in through our own living. However, death is also the opening of a chapter to the next stage of our journey. It opens us into a world that is not bound by place or time as we know it.

In an age where too many feel they are the holders of 'truth', this poem reminds us that God created each of us, in all of our diversity. It is God who will welcome us all: the strong and the weak, the arrogant and the meek, the wealthy and the poor of heart. He welcomes everyone, especially those who are broken and at the point of despair.

My soul is at ease when reading this poem; it reminds me in very few lines that the Hereafter is a place of solace, compassion and love. It brings me comfort to know that all those who have felt the pain of loved ones leaving for a better world can fathom that they are with the Most Merciful and the Most Kind.

As a child, I lost loved ones and felt the incredible pain this brought to my family and me. At the age of 12, I had little understanding of what would happen to those who left us and where they would be now. Growing older, I began to know God and came to understand the concept of the Hereafter as where life naturally proceeds.

Ultimately, God's message of love and peace ensures that we all feel worthy of His unconditional love and mercy. God himself encourages us to love ourselves enough to rid ourselves of the guilt and other material trappings that prevent us from seeing Him in this way. He loves and welcomes us all from wherever we may have travelled; for our travel is always towards death and it is at this point that this poem can bring strength and comfort to those who mourn the loss of their loved ones. It gives us an insight into a world that we know very little about and into which Rumi gives us eloquent glimpses through his poetry.

My belief in the Hereafter is important to me, along with my belief in a God who is loving, compassionate and forgiving. It is at the core of my understanding of the linear journey my soul is taking. Knowing my soul will move on and return to its Lord encourages and inspires me to try to know my Creator – although this can be a tricky task with my human limitations.

By coming to know myself, I come to know my Lord. Hence, I am able to make some sense of the journey of those who leave this world for the next. This helps me to comprehend life and death, and, most importantly, that our lives do not end but continue once we depart this world.

* * *

Sughra Ahmed is Senior Programmes Manager at the Woolf Institute where she specialises in research and training on the diversity of societies and the complex needs of public institutions when engaging with global faith relations. She studied English Language and Literature, has an MA in Islamic Studies and a Diploma in Islamic Jurisprudence. Sughra is Chair of the Islamic Society of Britain and a Trustee of the Inter Faith Network UK. (Twitter: @sughra01)

Dr Sarah Edelman

Clinical psychologist; President,
Dying with Dignity NSW

AUSTRALIA

Aina Ranke, the day before her death
Photo: Gideon Cordover

As a clinical psychologist, I occasionally see severely depressed individuals who are planning to end their lives. In these situations I pull out all stops to ensure their safety, including arranging hospitalisation if necessary. I know their perceptions are skewed by feelings of hopelessness and despair, and that this will change following successful treatment. While depression is transient, death is permanent, and suicide from treatable mental illness is indeed a tragedy.

However, in some circumstances the desire for death can be rational. Aina Ranke contacted the office of Dying with Dignity NSW in June 2013. She said that she was living with a progressive neuromuscular disease that was making her life unbearable. Aina had lost the ability to perform all but the most menial tasks and was struggling to talk, walk, feed herself or perform basic self-care. She told me that she planned to end her life in three days, and that she would like me to help her to tell her story.

Two days later I went to her home, and my colleague Gideon filmed our conversation. In spite of her difficulty with speech, Aina communicated eloquently. She described the daily frustrations of living with constant pain and disability, which had led to her decision to end her life. She had looked for a method that would be painless and peaceful, and managed to obtain the drug Nembutal.

Aina had chosen this time to die because she still had some control over the manner of her death. Given the potentially serious legal consequences of assisting a suicide, she decided not to involve friends. Nevertheless, she had not been secretive about her plan to end her life. During a recent stay at Maitland Hospital, she spoke openly about her decision to end her life. A psychiatric team was promptly sent to assess her. Their subsequent report concluded that Aina was of sound mind and was appraising her circumstances realistically.

It was impossible not to feel moved talking to this feisty, intelligent woman who was planning to be dead by the same time the following day. She seemed remarkably sanguine and calm. In her mind, dying was not the problem. It was the prospect of living on in her current circumstances that worried her. That she had a way out gave her a sense of control, and curtailed feelings of hopelessness.

The following day, I was horrified to be told that Aina had been found unconscious and had been resuscitated. She was now at the Mater Hospital on life support. In spite of extensive documentation expressing her wishes to the contrary, treatment was to proceed, subject to viability of life. Four days later, brain scans revealed extensive brain damage; consequently, life support was turned off.

Aina's case demonstrates the absurdity of compelling individuals suffering from awful degenerative illnesses to persevere against their will. Are we happy with laws that prohibit mentally competent adults with unrelievable suffering from being able to determine the manner and timing of their death? Or laws that make criminals of those who try to import drugs to enable them to die peacefully at a time of their choosing, and that would convict their loved ones if they tried to assist?

Every time our state parliaments vote down bills that seek to legalise voluntary assisted dying, they affect the lives of people like Aina, whose pain and suffering will only get worse over time. Currently, determined individuals are left to pursue illegal, sometimes unreliable, methods that can end in tragedy, as almost happened in Aina's case. If politicians are not prepared to listen, then it is up to those of us who care to remind them that our current laws are inhumane, and do not reflect the values of most Australians. When suffering is intolerable and unrelievable, a peaceful death at the time of one's choosing should be a basic human right.

* * *

Dr Sarah Edelman is President of Dying with Dignity NSW. She is also a clinical psychologist, author and trainer. Sarah's PhD was in psycho-oncology, and she became a passionate supporter of end-of-life choices while running therapy groups for women with advanced breast cancer. Sarah's book *Change Your Thinking* is a best-seller in the self-help genre.

Trypheyna McShane

Art therapist, storyteller and author

AUSTRALIA

I am standing upon the seashore. A ship at my side spreads her white sails to the morning breeze, and starts for the blue ocean.

She is an object of beauty and strength, and I stand and watch until at last she hangs like a speck of white cloud just where the sea and sky come down to mingle with each other. Then someone at my side says, 'There! She's gone!'

Gone where? Gone from my sight…that is all.

She is just as large in mast and hull and spar as she was when she left my side, and just as able to bear her load of living freight to the place of destination.

Her diminished size is in me, not in her.

And just at the moment when someone at my side says, 'There she goes!' there are other eyes watching her coming; and other voices ready to take up the glad shout: 'Here she comes!'

And that is – 'dying'.

Revd Luther F. Beecher, *What is Dying?*

Having spent time with people at end of life, the above passage speaks clearly to me about my sense of death. It helps remind us that we only *think* we know what the truth about death is.

I sense we are constantly being asked to rethink all our old paradigms of death and dying. Many more people are now comfortable talking about their near-death experiences. Others have witnessed conversations between those dying and those who have already died, both of which I have experienced. I no longer fear death and for this I am incredibly grateful.

We all leave a legacy, whether we realise it or not. My father John instilled in our family the love of sailing and the ocean as well as justice and truth. After he died, my mother Liz missed him so much that I offered to paint his portrait for her. I mixed his ashes into the paint and had a beautiful conversation with him while I was painting him. Liz kept the painting with her until she died, saying she loved knowing he was always with her.

As I contemplate my own death, I love the story of the Buddhist monks who turn their empty water glass upside down on going to sleep at night. This is their signal to those left behind that should they die during the night, they were absolutely ready for the journey. I love the idea that no matter what, and no matter where we are, we will be ready when it is our time to leave. This idea makes it more compelling for us to stay in the present, loving every moment of life as it unfolds.

I teach that everyone is an artist and it is through our creativity that our soul gets to speak. Memory making is an important aspect of our legacy, and vital for our ongoing connection to our families, ancestors and those yet to come.

* * *

Trypheyna McShane spent her early years in Ghana, Denmark and England, and lived on a yacht in the West Indies before arriving in Australia aged 19. As an artist, she has worked with young and old, Aboriginal communities, people with disabilities, wildlife and children at end of life. Trypheyna is co-author of *The Intimacy of Death and Dying: Simple Guidance to Help You Through*. (www. theendoflifematters.com)

Stephen Miller

Obituary writer

USA

Tribute in Lights, 9/11, 2013
Photo: © Eduard Moldoveanu/Dreamstime.com

Although I believe in a transcendent human spirit, I don't believe that souls exist in an individual sense. I think people live on in the memories of people they knew and people who knew of them. This makes writing obituaries an especially meaningful job for me. The lives of the living are immeasurably enriched by contemplating those who have departed.

I escaped unscathed from the 80th floor of the South Tower of the World Trade Center in the 9/11 attacks. A memorial displayed annually on 11 September serves as a dramatic image of lives remembered.

These two beams of light, giant spotlights, shoot up from the footprints of the old towers, visible for miles around New York City. The image is energy shooting into space, for all who survive to see. It feels to me like the human spirit returning to inhabit the universe. Those who have lived become part of the universe, transformed from a single thing into everything.

* * *

Stephen Miller is an obituary writer for Bloomberg News. He previously worked as an obituary writer at the *Wall Street Journal* and *New York Sun*, and before that he published his own obit magazine, *GoodBye* (www.goodbyemag.com). He has been a technician on Wall Street and did graduate studies in anthropology. He lives outside New York with his wife and son.

Dr Ian Gawler OAM

Buddhist cancer survivor; pioneer
in mind/body medicine
AUSTRALIA

The moment of death may be the greatest
moment of your life
It may be better than the best
chocolate sundae you ever had
It may be better than the best orgasm you ever had
It may be better than the dearest, happiest
moment you hold in your memory

For in that moment of death
The spirit separates from the body
And in that moment
It is free – totally free

If you can grasp that clear moment of death
Recognize it for what it is and experience it fully
Then you will experience fully who you really are
And unite with the mystery and essence of life itself

The only thing that scares me about the moment of death
Is that I may come to it unprepared

To be prepared for the moment of death
I would need to feel that I had lived fully
Loving and learning as much as I could during this
lifetime
And feeling free of regrets

To be prepared I would need to feel that
Those around me would be alright
That I could let go of my worldly attachments
And that they could release me

To be prepared
I would need to be free of fear
And to have had some glimpse of my own true nature –
Perhaps through the introduction of meditation

Being prepared for that clear moment of death
Then it may well be
That I would be able to recognize what I have been
searching for always –
The heart and essence of who I really am.

Ian Gawler, *The Clear Moment of Death*

Many people, it seems, do dread the prospect of death. Yet, so often, the fear of dying inhibits both healing and life itself. To reconcile death, to face it, to integrate it, to be ready to die, is to be ready to live fully. This is a feature of many cancer survivors with whom I have worked – they have faced death, moved through its domain and re-emerged to celebrate life.

Perhaps the most beautiful comment came from four-and-a-half-year-old Anna. When asked by her mother what she thought had happened when her grandmother died of cancer, Anna paused to reflect for a moment and then replied, 'Well, Mummy, just the *living part* went out of her.'

But even more than this, it may well be that in the moment of death all of our most profound questions about life and death are actually answered. We get to find out.

Maybe death could be a moment of delight, filled with clarity?

✳ ✳ ✳

Australian Buddhist Ian Gawler has played a major part in popularising meditation, mind/body medicine and other self-help techniques in the West. A former veterinarian and long-term cancer survivor, Ian co-founded the world's first lifestyle-based cancer and multiple sclerosis groups. Author of many books, including *You Can Conquer Cancer*, Ian is passionate about health, healing and wellbeing. He has also helped many people to die well. (www.iangawler.com)

Amelia Freelander

Media team, Amnesty International Australia

AUSTRALIA

#KeepHopeAlive installation and final vigil for Andrew Chan and Myuran Sukumaran, at Blues Point Reserve, Sydney, on Monday 27 April 2015

Photo: Amnesty International/Sitthixay Ditthavong

On 29 April 2015, in every corner of Amnesty International Australia's open-plan office, people were comforting each other. Some were in tears; others were sitting, solitary and quiet, at their desks.

This was a moment so many of us had hoped would never come. Two Australians, Andrew Chan and Myuran Sukumaran, and six others – Raheem Agbaje Salami, Zainal Abidin, Martin Anderson alias Belo, Rodrigo Gularte, Sylvester Obiekwe Nwolise and Okwudili Oyatanze – had been lined up, their hands tied to wooden slats, and shot.

Their deaths were all the more difficult to understand because this was no tragic accident or criminal act: it was state-sanctioned killing, on the orders of the Indonesian government.

Convicted of drug trafficking, both Andrew and Myuran had been sentenced to death after a criminal trial in 2006. Although Amnesty International campaigns against the death penalty in all cases, years of intense media coverage in Australia had seen us build an understanding and connection with the two young men, Andrew and Myuran. In the last nine years, we watched Andrew become a Christian pastor and Myuran a well-respected artist. We heard countless stories about how the two were influential in helping other inmates stay off drugs and had resolved to spend the rest of their days helping others. Their brutal executions seemed, and remain, futile.

Their deaths had followed loud and growing pleas for mercy, petitions, vigils, online pleas and calls which escalated even as their deaths loomed, and continued even after the 72-hour notice period of the executions taking place.

Even as the final hours loomed, thousands of Australians joined Amnesty International's *#FlowersOfHope* campaign. Over 10,000 flowers were purchased for an installation, and final vigil, held at Blues Point Reserve, Sydney, on Monday 27 April 2015. This striking image, shown here, with the message *#KeepHopeAlive* spelled out in flowers and candles, was emblazoned on the pages of news outlets in Australia, and overseas, including *The Jakarta Globe*.

By the time the news of their executions broke early on the morning of 29 April, there were many of us who had lain awake, eyes glued to the 24-hour news channel, waiting for what we hoped would be a last-minute reprieve.

It had been an intensely emotional three months and must have been absolutely harrowing for their families and friends, following the dismissal of requests for clemency from Indonesia's President that had been lodged years prior.

Despite moments of promise, on 29 April many Australians experienced the inhumanity and tragedy of the death penalty for the first time, as it was officially announced that the men we had grown to know and respect were now no longer with us.

Although personally crushed and devastated by their executions, my heart aches for their families and friends. Their complete devastation and this horrific act have only further bolstered my commitment to campaign against the death penalty. I will forever stand against this barbaric act.

But what we do know and we must not forget is that where there's hope, there's life. When Amnesty International started campaigning to abolish the death penalty in the 1970s, well before I was born, it must have seemed an impossible task. Only 16 countries had abolished it. Now over 30 years later, 140 countries have abolished it in law or practice. Until we live in a death-penalty-free world, the campaign to end state-sanctioned killing will continue, and even in the face of death, and in the throes of grief, we will remain united.

* * *

Atheist Amelia Freelander joined the media team at Amnesty International Australia in 2012 (www.amnesty.org. au). She works across the Refugee, End the Death Penalty and Asia-Pacific campaigns and was heavily involved in the campaign to secure the release of Andrew Chan and Myuran Sukumaran. Prior to Amnesty International, Amelia worked for seven years as a broadcast journalist at both public and commercial broadcasters.

Claire Henry MBE

Chief Executive, National Council for Palliative Care and the Dying Matters Coalition, England, Wales and Northern Ireland

UK

You can shed tears that she is gone
or you can smile because she has lived.
You can close your eyes and pray that she'll come back
or you can open your eyes and see all she's left.
Your heart can be empty because you can't see her
or you can be full of the love you shared.
You can turn your back on tomorrow and live yesterday
or you can be happy for tomorrow because of yesterday
You can remember her and only that she is gone
or you can cherish her memory and let it live on.
You can cry and close your mind,
be empty and turn your back
or can do what she'd want:
smile, open your eyes, love and go on.

David Harkins, *Remember Me*

This poem reflects the importance to me of remembering and not forgetting people that I have known and loved. As a colleague recently said, you want people to say their name and not forget them.

I have had the privilege to know and care for many incredible people, all providing me with important memories. The one who has had the greatest impact on me is my Grandma. Hence the poem. Remembering her and what she would have said brings strength to me in times of sadness. It is important to have time to reflect and release emotions, which enable me to carry on.

Good memories are the medicine of life for me as we are creating them on a daily basis. At the time we are totally unaware of the incredible impact and comfort these will bring after the person has died. I feel that laughter and tears go hand in hand with death, and I hope that my Grandma is looking and smiling down on me, knowing that I have my eyes wide open and am carrying on.

✳ ✳ ✳

Claire Henry is Chief Executive of the National Council for Palliative Care (www.ncpc.org.uk), which leads the Dying Matters Coalition (www.dyingmatters.org). Claire has had many experiences in both her professional life and personal life of dying, death and bereavement, which have shaped the way she views death.

Dr Colin Murray Parkes OBE

Consultant Psychiatrist, St Christopher's Hospice;
Life President, Cruse Bereavement Care

UK

> One short sleep past, we wake eternally
> And death shall be no more: death, thou shalt die.
>
> John Donne, *Death, be not proud*

Donne portrays the Christian promise that mind will survive matter. In fact, it is more likely the other way round. Matter will survive mind, for mind requires matter in order to survive, but matter does not depend on mind. Does that matter?

Of course, it may be that even the tiniest speck of matter does mind. I like to think of the perpetual Brownian movement of atoms as the manifestation of the Cosmic Dance. Instead of joining angelic choirs after death, we rejoin the celestial ballet from which we came.

Buddhists believe that in order to achieve nirvana we must surrender self. If, as I believe, the individual self disintegrates with death, the acceptance of that destiny may lead to a peaceful death.

But in every moment of every day of our lives we are permanently changing the world, for better or worse. It follows that although the 'I' dies, the effect of each life does not. Indeed, viewed in that way, we all live on forever. We live on in the consequences of our lives and we need to take responsibility for those consequences while we can. Part of that responsibility is to look after our own bodies. We multi-cellular organisms must stick together.

Perhaps it is *life*, with its cell walls, skin and locked doors, that separates us from each other, *not death*. When we die, the boundaries dissolve and we become reunited with the universal life.

For many years I have been comforted by the thought that I shall be ready to die when I have finished life, 'been there, done that, nothing new under the sun'. Or, as one of my patients said, 'I am full up with life and don't want a second helping'. There is an element of truth in this: I already find myself losing my appetite for life, less inclined to travel long distances to visit new places.

In biological terms, I started dying years ago. When I cannot remember the name of an old friend, I experience the consequences of losing brain cells. But those brain cells sent me no sensory awareness of their dying.

There is another side to this coin. Paradoxically, rather than running out of surprises, life seems to be full of them. This may result from the loss of memory that is a part of growing old. Sometimes, in the eyes of the very, very old, we catch sight of a person who, like every newborn baby, gazes with amazement at a world completely new.

The nearest I can get to an image of death is of a comedian saying 'And now for something completely different' and a great curtain opens or a cloak falls away...

✳ ✳ ✳

Pantheist Dr Colin Murray Parkes is Emeritus Consultant Psychiatrist to St Christopher's Hospice, London, where he set up the first hospice-based bereavement service. He is Life President of Cruse Bereavement Care and author of many books on bereavement. More recently, Colin has worked with communities dealing with trauma, including Rwanda, New York after 9/11 and, following the major tsunamis, India and Japan.

The Reverend Jonathan Woodhouse CB

Baptist minister; former Chaplain-General of the British Army

UK

So I saw in my dream that they [pilgrims Christian and Hopeful] went on together till they came in sight of the gate. Now I further saw that between them and the gate was a river, but there was no bridge to go over and the river was very deep. At the sight, therefore, of this river, the pilgrims were much stunned...

They were told, 'you shall find it deeper or shallower, as you believe in the King of the place...'

Then I saw in my dream that Christian was in a muse a while, and the words came, 'When you pass through the waters I will be with you; and through the rivers they shall not overflow you' [Isaiah 43:2]. Then they took courage...until they were gone over...

Then I heard in my dream that all the bells in the city rang again for joy and that it was said to them, 'Enter into the joy of our Lord.'

John Bunyan, *The Pilgrim's Progress*

As an army chaplain, I have read these words by John Bunyan in the quietness of my study and the noise of a desert war. In both places, the picture of crossing the river (of death) reminds me not only of the inevitability of my own mortality but also of the final struggle of adversity before reaching the far bank. I like to think it will be in old age but I have seen enough young people die to know this may not be so. The dream is vivid. It portrays a very human measure of fear and struggle alongside a divine measure of hope and rest in reaching firm ground on the other side.

I have reflected on my mortality in the predictability of ordinary routine and in the utter unpredictability of living on the edge during military operations where comfort is stripped away and life becomes basic and stark. These reflections led me to feel I was 'trusted with bringing the Hope of God' to soldiers and their families during my tenure as Chaplain General.

My Baptist forebear, John Bunyan, lived in one of the most unpredictable and turbulent periods in English history with the Civil War, the Great Plague, the Great Fire of London included. His famous allegory touches me at a deep level in what I believe is an even more turbulent and dangerous world. The final barrier is the river. Laying my burden down on the bank is one thing. Crossing the river is another. Whether that crossing is swift and simple or long and tiring, I will have to cross it. Christian (the pilgrim) is anxious at the fast-flowing current with a walk on foot and the fear of being swept away even with the far side of the bank in view.

Christian hope should never ignore the mystery and power of death. This river is always flowing and waiting as the last enemy for the pilgrim. There is no bridge over it or detour around it. 'I dare you to step in,' it says. One day, I will.

The Pilgrim's Progress is honest in admitting to the fear this can hold but it also points to the far side of the river and the hope which Christian faith brings in helping to cross the final divide.

Recently, I was with my mother as she stepped into this river and, as Christian experienced in Bunyan's allegory, I believe the bells in the city on the far bank rang for joy as she reached the other side. With all the mystery around death, this river, even in full flood, is not the end. With God in Christ, Bunyan's picture of the river shows that death is a comma, not a full stop. Here is my hope on my pilgrim journey.

* * *

Jonathan Woodhouse is a Baptist minister and army chaplain. He served in Germany, Cyprus, Hong Kong, the Falkland Islands, the Royal Military Academy Sandhurst, Iraq and Afghanistan. Jonathan was appointed Chaplain-General of the British Army in 2011 and retired in 2014. He has received many awards and was appointed Companion of the Order of the Bath in the 2014 Queens Birthday Honours.

Caitlin Doughty

Mortician; Founder, Order of the Good Death

USA

…the face of death is green,
and the gaze of death green…

Pablo Neruda, *Selected Poems*

The face of death is green.

Poetic, but death cannot be green. Death is a *man*, and he is *skeletal*. That is our Death in the Western world. He is the Grim Reaper with his scythe and robes, underneath which his bones are picked clean. It's quite sterile that way. He is a tidy killer – medical, even.

'It would be obscene to make him green, to paint his face like a clown. Death is not a whimsical character from Dr Seuss!' you say.

Please join me in reimagining our death in the West. Drop the outdated idea of death as a clean, sterilised man. *Death is a woman*, green, smelling of rich soil and earth. Death is where we came from and where we will all return.

For my own sanity, as a secular person, death must be as green as the earth. When I die, I must sink my body back into the soil, because that is the only sacred I know. I must give back myself over as food for literal worms in payment for what I've taken all my life. And how I've taken, how we've all taken. My corpse will not be a worthy enough gift, but I will give it. I hope the animals and the grass and the trees enjoy the banquet of my flesh.

* * *

Caitlin Doughty is a licensed mortician and the host and creator of the 'Ask a Mortician' web series. She founded the death acceptance collective the Order of the Good Death (www.orderofthegooddeath.com) and co-founded Death Salon. She lives in Los Angeles where she owns an alternative funeral home, Undertaking LA.

Bruce Kent

Peace activist; Vice-President, Campaign for Nuclear Disarmament and Pax Christi UK

UK

Dark brown is the river.
Golden is the sand.
It flows along for ever,
With trees on either hand.

Green leaves a-floating,
Castles of the foam,
Boats of mine a-boating –
Where will all come home?

On goes the river
And out past the mill,
Away down the valley,
Away down the hill.

Away down the river,
A hundred miles or more,
Other little children
Shall bring my boats ashore.

Robert Louis Stevenson, *Where Go the Boats?*

This haunting four-verse poem has a wonderful last verse. It expresses my understanding of death. We are all children in this world. We are in or on the river of life, playing with our boats. Foolish to think we have some permanence! The time will come when we will all hand our hopes and dreams on to future generations.

My 'preparation for death' is to suggest that I am doing this all the time. Not really. I am aware as I get older – and I am now in my eighties – that the clock is ticking, but I am not sitting down daily contemplating the future. I do say the Lord's Prayer to myself much more often than before: 'Thy Kingdom Come, Thy Will be done...' And, in my own small way, I am trying to still make that happen as much now as, I hope, in past years. I believe that our commitment to compassion for others is the love of God squeezing its way out of us into the world.

What lies beyond? I have almost no idea. We are like ants crawling across the top of a computer. We have no idea or understanding of the source of all the wonders of the vast and amazing world we crawl across. And as for the future, I like to think that my little candle is heading into a searchlight of brilliance beyond my dreams.

* * *

Bruce Kent was educated in Canada and England, served in the Army 1947–1949, was ordained a priest in 1958 and retired in 1987. His peace and justice initiatives include General Secretary and Chairperson of the Campaign for Nuclear Disarmament (CND) 1980–1990, Chair of War on Want and President of the International Peace Bureau. Currently, he is Vice-President of CND and Pax Christi UK.

FURTHER VERSES

A salt doll journeyed for thousands of miles over land, until it finally came to the sea. It was fascinated by this strange moving mass, quite unlike anything it had ever seen before.

'Who are you?' said the salt doll to the sea.

The sea smilingly replied, 'Come in and see.'

So the doll waded in. The farther it walked into the sea the more it dissolved, until there was only very little of it left. Before that last bit dissolved, the doll exclaimed in wonder, 'Now I know what I am! We are one.'

Anthony de Mello, The Salt Doll

Take care with the end as you do with the beginning.

Attributed to Lao Tzu

For life and death are one, even as the river and the sea are one.

Kahlil Gibran, The Prophet

PART 5

Death Is Sacred

How is death understood within different cultures and faith traditions? Although Part 5 may echo some sentiments in previous reflections, these contributors share their underlying beliefs which help guide them in understanding and accepting the mystery of death. Connections to the Divine, belief in life's sanctity, the transition of the soul to eternal life through death, and the return of our essence to the source of life are all expressions of wisdom included here.

A peace activist from El Salvador and a village elder from Papua New Guinea present their cultural perspectives about death. We hear voices too from different faith traditions including an artist and social activist, a Bahá'í author, a Christian palliative care physician, a Tibetan Buddhist nun, a peace and social activist, a Brahma Kumaris peace emissary, a community rabbi, a Sikh visionary religious leader, a Hindu interfaith practitioner, a Gomeroi Aboriginal man and a research consultant who is a practising Jehovah's Witness.

Their sentiments include:

'...death is not the end but the
beginning of an everlasting life.'

'...death is nothing more than another "stop"
in the long journey of my *Ātma* [Soul]...'

'Our journey from birth to death makes
us all, in a way, migrant travellers.'

'The Bible refers to death as simply being asleep.'

'My understanding and experience
is that the soul is eternal.'

Dr Pushpa Bhardwaj-Wood

Hindu interfaith practitioner

NEW ZEALAND

Just as a person discards old and worn out garments in order to put on new garments, similarly, the eternal *Ātma* or soul gives up old and worn out physical bodies to accept new physical bodies.

The soul cannot be cut by any weapon nor can it be harmed, the fire cannot burn the soul, nor can water wet it and air cannot dry up the soul – in other words while the soul resides in a destructible body, it is by nature indestructible.

Bhagavad Gita 2:22–23

As a Hindu, when I die, I would like to be cremated. My basic philosophy and understanding is that by the action of cremation, all five elements are reunited – fire, water, air, ether and earth. In essence, the act of cremation reinforces the concept of detachment.

Death essentially separates the Soul (which is eternal) from the material body (which is destructible). To me, death is nothing more than another 'stop' in the long journey of my *Ātma* (Soul) to be reunited with *Paramātmā* (Supreme Soul). A transitory phase to the next stage.

I deeply believe that I was sent on this earth with a specific purpose and my quest has been to identify that purpose and fulfil it to the best of my ability. I also know that when my job is done, it will be time to leave – regardless! The date, time and place for my ultimate departure from this material world are predetermined and I do not see any point in worrying about something that is beyond my control. However, I do believe in being prepared – you never know when this 'invitation' will arrive.

Besides the Vedas, the Bhagavad Gita has been the other most influential text in my life. I have always found the second chapter, *The Eternal Reality of the Soul's Immortality*, in particular the above two *shlokas* (verses), to be most reassuring.

* * *

Indian-born Pushpa Bhardwaj-Wood, a Hindu, moved to New Zealand in 1980. A founding member of the interfaith movement in New Zealand, she has participated in many Asia-Pacific Regional Interfaith forums including an award-winning exhibition on 'Death and Diversity' at the Museum of Wellington City and Sea. Pushpa's lifelong dream is to utilise religion as a uniting force for humanity.

Sharifah Zuriah Aljeffri

Artist and social activist

MALAYSIA

Bismillha Rahmani Rahim
(In the name of Allah the Most Gracious, the Most Merciful)
Photo: Sharifah Zuriah Aljeffri

In the name of Allah, Most Gracious, Most Merciful.
Praise be to Allah, The Cherisher and
Sustainer of the Worlds;
Most Gracious, Most Merciful;
Master of the Day of Judgement.
Thee we do worship, and Thine aid we seek.
Show us the straight way,
The way of those on whom
Thou has bestowed Thy Grace,
Those whose (portion) is not wrath, and who do not go astray.

The Qur'an 1:1–7 (*Al-Fatihah*)

Al-Fatihah reminds me that my life on earth is temporary
and that death is not the end but the beginning of an

179

everlasting life. One day I will meet my Creator and I will be answerable to Him for my actions on earth. God will judge us not for our wealth but for our faith and deeds. We do not know when we will die and whether we will go to paradise or to hell. Only God knows. We pray to God to guide us on the straight way that will lead us to heaven and not to hell.

Even though I am aware that I will one day die, I never realised that the people I love would also be gone. My first experience of death, which greatly affected me emotionally, was hearing the news of my father's passing while I was studying overseas in London. I was devastated and the first thing I did was recite the *Al-Fatihah* and other short *surahs* (chapters) from the Qur'an. Then I prayed that his soul was at peace and he was among believers.

I also read surah *Ya Sin* (Qur'an 36:1–83) for him. This is considered the heart of the Qur'an and is usually recited over the dying person. His death affected me so much that I would cry myself to sleep and was afraid to go out. I began to read surah *Ya Sin* every day, which gave me solace. That was 51 years ago and I still miss him. There are many other passages in the Qur'an mentioning death and the Day of Judgement including 'Every human being is bound to taste death.' (*Al-Imran* 3:185).

When a person is dying, he or she will be guided to say the *Shahadah* (the Islamic Creed and the first of the five pillars of Islam): 'There is no god but God and Prophet Mohammed is the messenger of God.'

My mother passed away in 2012 after a short illness. May her soul rest in peace. She was 98 years old. In her last days, I would read surahs *Al-Fatihah* and *Ya Sin* and whisper in her ear the *Shahadah*, so that she could repeat it after me. I hoped it would ease her pain and discomfort as she prepared to meet God. I miss her very much.

When I recite the *Al-Fatihah*, I imagine myself talking to God. Remembering God through prayers, supplications and reading the Qur'an gives me the greatest comfort, peace and inner strength especially in times of sadness or illness.

* * *

Zuriah is a Malaysian cultural advisor, artist, environmentalist and social activist. She is a founding member and former Coordinator of Sisters in Islam (SIS). Her iconic Arabic calligraphy paintings reflect her spiritual contemplation and her interpretation of socio-political issues, including war atrocities. Zuriah's paintings also reflect and explore people's relationship with nature.

Sr Jayanti

European Director, Brahma Kumaris; peace emissary

UK

Thank You
Thank you for your inspiration
For your life and love
Thank you for your recognition of the one above
Thank you for your sweet compassion
for your life of truth
Thank you for walking on this earth
Thank you for being you

The River flows back to the Ocean,
the trees turn back to dust
The sun must set as the day it ends
And so shall all of us
The gift of silence is returned to each one soul by soul
I know you feel it in your heart as
you watch your life unfold

So go to the sea
Flow to the Ocean
Fly like a bird to His arms
Take all the love of all who will miss you
But know we are never apart

Lucinda Drayton, *Bliss*

My mother began meditating with the Brahma Kumaris when I was eight, so I grew up with the influence of meditation and spirituality. In 2001, when she passed away, a fellow meditator, Lucinda Drayton, wrote a song in her honour and sang it at her cremation. Lucinda wrote that she felt deep gratitude for those who use their lives to serve. My mother's faith in God was central in her life and influenced the whole family.

My understanding and experience is that the soul is eternal. It never dies. It simply passes from one bodily costume to another. To remember a departed one as a human being brings sorrow. By remembering the *soul* in the awareness of God, we can send thoughts of God's love and light that reach the soul. Seeing death as a natural transition into another state removes fear and we can respond more calmly.

The soul's strongest relationship is to the body, so understandably there's trauma around leaving it. A meditation practice that prepares us for leaving is 'soul consciousness': experiencing the self as a being of light, detached from the body. Being aware of the soul and its intrinsic goodness, we start to perform actions based on our original nature of purity, peace, love, truth and joy. We let go of past pain and unhelpful habits and move forward. We experience freedom. When it's time to leave, we know it's not the end.

At the time of transition (death), God's remembrance supports the soul, giving the experience of flying to the Light to God. In meditation, we experience God's love, power and guidance; this prepares us for staying connected to God in our final moments.

This is a life journey. The destination is to be at one with God but the journey itself can only be with God as our Companion.

* * *

Sr Jayanti is the European Director of Brahma Kumaris World Spiritual University and their representative to the United Nations, Geneva (www.brahmakumaris.org). For 45 years she has been an emissary for peace, travelling internationally as a speaker and broadcaster. She sees the erosion of spiritual values as the underlying cause of the crises facing today's world.

Bhai Sahib Bhai (Dr) Mohinder Singh Ahluwalia

Religious Leader and Chair, Guru Nanak Nishkam Sewak Jatha (GNNSJ)

UK

1. Heerey jaisaa janam hai, kaudee badle jaaey...
Like a precious diamond is our human birth into this world;
Let us not waste it, as if it were worth mere cowrie shells.

2. Jeevat marai dargeh parvaan...
When one accomplishes the art of remaining 'dead
whilst still alive'
And lives free from ego's negative grip,
Such a person earns a place in the Divine Court.

*3. Aagey kaou kichh tulhaa baandhoh,
kiaa bharvaasaa dhan ka...*
So plan ahead and build a raft for the voyage across life's
worldly ocean –
This will help you, both in the here and now and the hereafter.
Place not your faith in perishable possessions,
for they will be of no avail.

*4. Jin nirbhau, jin har nirbhau dhiaaiaa
jee, tin kaa bhau sabh gavaasee...*
Only those who attune themselves to the Fearless One,
Will have their fear (of death) dispelled.

*5. Sooraj kiran milai, jal ka jal hooaa raam;
Jyoti jyot ralee, sampooran theea raam...*
Just as sunrays can merge back into the sun,
And droplets of water merge back into the ocean,
So should one's inner light merge with the Divine Light,
And therein find wholeness complete.

Sri Guru Granth Sahib Ji

These verses from Sri Guru Granth Sahib Ji – the sacred text revered by Sikhs as 'living' Eternal Guru – convince us that the gift of human life is our most precious and divine asset. Such a life must be wisely and passionately lived, valued and safeguarded. It should also be directed towards serving the Creator and all creation. Since childhood, I have sung, recited and listened to these melodic teachings. Now that I am in my seventies, they continue to inspire and fill me with optimism. Translations are a poor substitute for the original, but I have endeavoured to convey a few chosen verses translated here in English, as a starting point for reflection.

The many references to death in Sri Guru Granth Sahib Ji urge us all to wake up and harness our full potential, instead of wasting golden opportunities and ending our days in regret. This is the gist of the first verse. From a Sikh perspective, the opportunity is golden because human birth offers a unique chance to ignite the divine spark latent within us. This involves mobilising spiritual attributes such as compassion, contentment, wisdom, courage, love and forgiveness, which enable us to live in God's image.

The challenge before us all is *haumai*. This is our inherent selfish 'ego' – an acronym, you could say, for 'edging God out', because it can cause us to lose a sense of the vast and infinite context of our lives. We become 'fully alive' when, for all intents and purposes, we become 'dead' unto ourselves – that is, by overcoming this overpowering *haumai*. Freed from ego, we have the potential to be spiritually liberated in the here and now, before our physical death. This idea is introduced in the second verse.

Our journey from birth to death makes us all, in a way, migrant travellers. Sikhs understand this as part of a greater voyage of the spirit. Upon death, the body perishes and disintegrates. Just as it was once composed, it starts to decompose. While we were living, our *haumai*'s negative forces – the likes of greed, arrogance and hate – had posed as our great friends and allies, ever shadowing and influencing us. At the moment of death, they disappear from the scene, like traitors. All that is left is the indestructible spirit, wrapped in layers created by our accumulated thoughts, actions and deeds. As we depart from this earthly sojourn, there are no material souvenirs we can take. We do, however, carry forward an 'essence' determined by the virtues and values we lived by. And so the second and third verses advise us of the need to prepare for the bigger journey ahead.

The subject of death is often approached with trepidation. Although we can marvel at life, we keenly fear its consequence. All creation, the sacred teachings describe – from the sun and the moon to the rivers and the wind – operate with a measure of fear. It is part of the awe and the wonder in which everything exists. Only the sole Creator is *nirbhau*, free from fear, and *nirvair*, free from enmity – and thus the source of all love. The fourth verse advises us that the only way to bypass our fear is to connect up with the One who is fearless and all-loving.

In my own life, I have known fear and pain, confusion and helplessness resulting from death. Living in Kenya as the youngest sibling, I was aged four years and seven months when my beloved mother passed away. She had been ill in hospital and it was there on the twentieth day that she told me, calling me 'Mindi' as she always did, that tomorrow she would be going away. She hugged and kissed me over and over again with tears in her eyes. A family friend of my own age told me of her passing on; my dear, heartbroken father could not bring himself to tell me so. Thus, from this tender age, questions about death and the purpose of life began to intrigue and haunt me. Ultimately, they set me on my own lifelong search.

I find great peace, solace and a sense of fulfilment in the fifth quote, which is often sung to mark the death of loved ones. This verse expresses the idea that the soul or spirit, like myriad aspects of nature, longs to connect with its root or origin; like the rays of the sun or droplets of water, it finally merges back into its source. This ultimate phenomenon of final unity, complete emancipation and oneness with Almighty God can help us embrace life and death positively, by striving to mobilise the best within us each day – and to prepare for the final breaths we will take one day.

We can never actually be sure as to when we will depart, for life and death are only a breath apart. Perhaps, then, we should each endeavour to write, in advance, our own obituary, to take stock of our life's battles and set out our enduring hopes. To do so would be a sobering, stabilising and poignant exercise.

* * *

Bhai Sahib Bhai (Dr) Mohinder Singh Ahluwalia is Religious Leader and Chair of the Nishkam Group of charitable organisations based in Birmingham, UK. His visionary, hands-on leadership is recognised through many prestigious national and international accolades and roles. His passion lies in stimulating value-centred, social innovation and community participation to positively transform local and global life. His unending source of inspiration is the 500-year eternal legacy of the Sikh faith – Guru Granth Sahib Ji.

Peter Shine

Gomeroi Aboriginal man from New South Wales; Director of Aboriginal Health, Northern Sydney Local Health District

AUSTRALIA

Please be aware that this contribution may contain the images and names of Aboriginal and Torres Strait Islander people who may have passed away.

Tell me where you're going Dad
And why you won't return
Your sickness makes me very sad
Is there more for me to learn?

I feel the pain you're going through
I see it in your face
But I don't know where you're going to
Is it a far off place?

They are calling Yurrandaali son
To live my life elsewhere
Baayami comes to take me son
You need not have a care

I will be here forever son
Especially in your soul
Yurrandaali Dreaming little one
Never growing old.

Peter Shine, *Yurrandaali (Tree Goanna) Dreaming*

The verses from the poem above have a particular meaning for me as an Aboriginal man. They talk about Baayami the Creator, Yurrandaali, my Aboriginal name or totem, and The Dreaming, which is where my people go when their life on this earth is over. These verses also capture part of a conversation between an Aboriginal man and his son; the son recognises that his father has a sickness and must go to a 'far off place'; the father assures the son that he will be with him from his Dreaming Place forever.

Death is a sacred and sad time for Aboriginal people. Death is referred to as Sorry Business by the family and clan of the deceased person and is a time of both mourning and celebration. My people (Gomeroi, Kamilaroi, Gamilaroi, Gumeroi) believe that Sorry Business is a part of life and that life and death are a part of the cycle of spirituality. In some Aboriginal communities, mentioning the deceased person's name or showing a photograph of them is considered offensive. Hence it is standard practice to make the above reference that 'this contribution may contain the images and names of Aboriginal and Torres Strait Islander people who may have passed away'. There is no definitive time limit on this practice.

Although Sorry Business is a sad time for my people, it can also be a celebration of the person's life *after* death. We believe that if they have been a good person on his or her 'country', then they will continue to live in The Dreaming as a good person or whatever incarnation Baayami chooses for them.

Sometimes Baayami allows the person to return to their country as their totem animal to be closer to family and clan. It is for this reason that my people are not allowed to eat their totem animal for fear it may be their loved one reincarnated.

We do not fear death; rather, we view it as the beginning of a closer relationship with Baayami and another part of our spiritual journey. My people believe very much that we are all bound to each other in a spiritual way. Aboriginal people have the view, as did John Donne in his poem *No Man is an Island*, that we are all diminished by the death or departing of another person's spirit.

> No man is an island entire of itself…
> …any man's death diminishes me,
> because I am involved in mankind.

My people are sustained by our belief in The Dreaming. Although there is no written evidence to support this belief, for over 60,000 years our people have lived with it to guide them and have handed it on to each generation. We believe that we are travelling spirits on this earth and that in The Dreaming Place our spiritual journey continues.

Gorialla Dreaming

Gorialla is one of many names across Aboriginal Australia attributed to the Rainbow Serpent. The circular motion of the swirl is representative of the never-ending circle of life in Aboriginal beliefs.

Photo: Peter Shine, 2005

* * *

Peter Shine is a Gomeroi man from north-western NSW, Australia. He has been involved in Aboriginal health and social and emotional wellbeing for many years. Peter is currently Director of Aboriginal Health, Northern Sydney Local Health District, and a Clinical Associate Professor at the Australian Catholic University. He lives in outer Western Sydney with his wife Jo, a Women's Health Nurse Practitioner.

Rabbi Sylvia Rothschild

Community rabbi; author; specialist in preparing liturgies for end-of-life experiences

UK

Judaism commonly talks of life as if it is vegetation. We talk about life as being like a tree, with branches growing as life goes on, with roots reaching far into the past and a crown reaching ever upward. A tree adds branches, it goes through the seasons and cycles of growth, good times and bad, times of blossom and of fruitfulness, times when death is near. The image is an organic one, a picture of slow growth, of development, of becoming something more as time goes on, and ultimately it bespeaks death, as, whether it be a blade of grass or a cedar of Lebanon, time takes its toll and we pay the ultimate price.

But there is another image in Judaism, the image of life as a precious jewel. And, like a jewel this image reminds us that every quality that we will have, we have had from the very beginning. Life does not add to our essence, it merely reveals who we already are. As we move through the years, facets may be enhanced or brought out, but the jewel already contained them and more. It is a different picture from the organic model of life, and it is, I think, far more true.

All of us know that when a child is born she is not a *tabula rasa* [a blank slate], on which we can project or engrave our expectations – she is a person in her own right, with a personality and identity of her own. She is a jewel, and living will simply polish the facets, or bring them out and add lustre to them – when a child is born she is already who she will be. Every quality is already present, every potential exists, and the essential person exists in all her complexity right now. The image of life as a tree can sometimes cause us insoluble problems, for a tree cut down before its time is wasted; the abrupt ending causes it to be lost and its possibilities to simply no longer exist. But a jewel that has been dropped in the grass remains a jewel, all its qualities are intact, it is simply that it has become lost to our sight.

Rabbi Rodney Mariner, *Movement for Reform Judaism (MRJ) Funeral Service Book*

I love this passage because it speaks essentially of the soul: that when we come into the world, our soul is already whole, and while experience may bring out characteristics, we are who we are and neither life nor death can change this.

The passage was written by a colleague, based on a number of Chasidic stories, and used originally for the funeral service of a young woman very involved in our community, whose fight against cancer touched many of us.

The charity she set up to help others like herself continues to reflect some of the gleam of the person she was. The image of a jewel dropped into the grass, unseen and unfound however hard we look, yet still there and intact, with the possibility of being found in the future, is comforting for the mourner. It holds out hope that death is not the end, that the person is not extinguished and we may find them again one day.

* * *

Rabbi Sylvia Rothschild has been a community rabbi in the UK since gaining *semicha* from Leo Baeck College in 1987.

She has written extensively on ethical issues and on prayer, and is known for her creation of a large number of new rituals and prayers including liturgies to help with end-of-life experiences. (www.rabbisylviarothschild.wordpress.com)

Dr Doreen Tembo

Research consultant in public health

UK

Do not go gentle into that good night,
Old age should burn and rave at close of day;
Rage, rage against the dying of the light.

Though wise men at their end know dark is right,
Because their words had forked no lightning they
Do not go gentle into that good night.

Good men, the last wave by, crying how bright
Their frail deeds might have danced in a green bay,
Rage, rage against the dying of the light.

Wild men who caught and sang the sun in flight,
And learn, too late, they grieved it on its way,
Do not go gentle into that good night.

Grave men, near death, who see with blinding sight,
Blind eyes could blaze like meteors and be gay,
Rage, rage against the dying of the light.

And you, my father, there on the sad height,
Curse, bless, me now with your fierce tears, I pray.
Do not go gentle into that good night.
Rage, rage against the dying of the light.

Dylan Thomas, *Do Not Go Gentle into that Good Night*

Although Dylan Thomas, in his famous poem, laments with rage the passing of men of varying life experiences in his first five stanzas, it is his very personal experience of his own father's end of life, in the sixth stanza, that inspires the passion and rage against death and loss.

Being involved with HIV/AIDS treatment in developing countries in the 1990s exposed me often to suffering and death. I have also encountered death personally when my 13-year-old eldest brother died in a car accident in 1988. This poem echoes the rage I felt.

As a Jehovah's Witness, I am also active in sharing and encouraging Bible-based spiritual thoughts and teachings about life and death within my community. So I do not worry about my own mortality. The Bible refers to death as simply being asleep (John 11:11). I believe we remain in God's memory although we rest in the grave. My anxiety about death is more for those I leave behind who will grieve for me. In turn, I fear the loss of those whom I love.

The raw pain of the loss of a loved one can shake one's faith, even with the knowledge that while God allows us to suffer and to die, he is not the cause of suffering or death (James 1:13 and Romans 5:12). In such times I do rage, and often the resentment is directed towards a God that does allow death to happen.

'It will get better with time' is a common phrase that is never appreciated, especially when our loss is new. But although our best efforts may fail to make the pain easier to bear, time inevitably does heal. Life rebuilds itself around a new configuration without the pieces we held so dear.

Once the anger and rage subside, God, the Bible, friends and family with similar beliefs give us much hope for the future in being reunited with our loved ones in a world without death and suffering.

* * *

Born in Zambia and a Jehovah's Witness, Doreen Tembo has lived in many countries with different mythologies, cultures and beliefs about dying and death, including Japan, Egypt and currently the UK. She specialised in HIV/AIDS global health policy in Zambia and Uganda for both her MSc and doctorate. Currently, Doreen offers consultancy services in research design for patient and public health involvement. (www.jw.org)

Reverend Marta Benavides

Christian social justice activist

EL SALVADOR

*Altar with photographs of my parents
at the El Museo Aja, Santa Ana*
Photo: Anna Rooney

This reflection is based on my life experiences, including times when I have been close to death. It has also been shaped by the teachings of my dear parents who are deceased. You can see the photographs of my mother Eva and father Theodore at their altar at the *El Museo Aja* (Aha Museum of Folk Cultures and Arts) in Santa Ana, El Salvador.

I am the oldest of four girls. I was born and raised in Cuscatlan, which means, in *Nahuatl*, 'land of riches', the indigenous peoples' name for El Salvador. Our family is of indigenous background, the First Nations of this land, the *Nahuat Pipil*. Although most of our people here are Christian (due to Spanish conquistadors), we still hold on to our indigenous roots and cultures very strongly. We call this our 'cosmo vision'.

When my sisters and I were young kids, we used to sit at the 'curve' in front of our house and tell scary stories. We got frightened, especially when going to bed, for it was all about ghosts and the dead – they were coming to get us! Our mom then explained to us that death is part of life; that everything in the universe is eternal, including us; that we are here, just on borrowed time; that we must live as though we are always ready to leave *Pachamama* (Mother Earth), for we never know for how long we will be here. She told us that there is no reason to fear death or dying. Rather, we must be mindful of how we live each day and each moment, for we have been born to live a life of plenitude, a useful life and one full of meaning. This must be our 'prayer in action' always.

In our continent of *Pachamama*, *Abya Yala*, we are mindful of this. We do not celebrate Halloween, but on 1 and 2 November we celebrate The Day of the Dead, a time to commemorate relatives, friends and ancestors. The first day is for the children who are no longer with us; the second day is for adults. Altars and cemeteries are decorated with photos of the deceased as well as food, flowers, perfume and music that our loved ones enjoyed in life. Their life is now eternal. We also place messages of peace and reconciliation in war-torn areas. They symbolise our dreams for a quality life and for a world order that honours all life on this loving planet.

Throughout my life I have deliberately chosen a path of working for peace and human rights for all. Consequently, I have risked my life during military dictatorships, coups d'état and detention, as well as from natural disasters such as earthquakes. These times of danger were heightened when I chose to accompany Archbishop Oscar Romero, who was martyred in 1980 for his ministry to the exploited, alienated and oppressed. I stand with those who suffer impoverishment and marginalisation, and take care of Mother Earth. This 'prayer in action' gives direction and purpose to my life.

* * *

Activist Marta Benavides was born in El Salvador, where she is a theologian, ordained minister, permaculturist and artist. Within the United Nations, Marta works for peace, environmental stability, sustainability, the equality of women and First Nations. She worked with Archbishop Oscar Romero in defending human rights and has founded a folk art museum, an eco house, free universities and a permaculture farm.

Dr Frank Brennan

Palliative Care Specialist,
Calvary Hospital

AUSTRALIA

By now the story was familiar. The familiarity did not ease the sorrow. That such a thing could be was inexplicable. And in that inexplicability lay the depth of sorrow. He was twenty-eight years old. A new man. Forming. His origins were Macedonia. He was a serious man. He was married and had no children. His father had died only a few months before. Suddenly. The family was still reeling in their grief.

His admission to the hospital had been prolonged. Multiple investigations, surgery, sepsis, long courses of antibiotics. The last scan was bitter news. The tide of any hope for cure had gone out. He was becoming much weaker. Each day the women sat by his bed. Their eyes down. His wife, his mother and his mother-in-law. In mourning for her husband, his mother was always dressed in black. She rarely looked up. One day when I asked them whether they had any questions for me, his mother sighed, looked at me directly and asked: 'Why?'

With the ultimate aim of home in mind he was transferred to the hospice to gain some time and, possibly, some strength. At first he and his family were disoriented – no intravenous fluids, no regular checks on his temperature, blood pressure and pulse. A scene of quiet compared to the hospital months. With explanation they settled.

One morning I was asked to see him urgently. He was distressed. Two senior nurses accompanied me.

When we entered his room I could sense a change. He had deteriorated since I'd last seen him. His mother sat beside his bed, her hand resting on his, her head down. I sat next to him. We talked about what he was feeling – emotional, anxious, even bewildered. He spoke in a whisper. He paused and, turning to look at me, asked me what I thought. As gently as I could I reflected on the change in his condition. We could all see this. I said that things were becoming harder. I said that I thought that his time was coming. He looked up at the ceiling, then towards me and asked: 'What do you mean by that?' I replied: 'Soon, Paul, you are going to die.'

Immediately his mother, as though stung, leapt up from her chair turned in a small circle screamed out and flung herself on him. 'No, Paul, you won't die. Your father's gone and not this. You will live until you are eighty-six years old.' She sat sobbing, her head on his hand, kissing his fingers, whispering over and over 'You can't go, you will live until you are eighty-six.' Paul looked up and said quietly: 'Comfort her.' One of the senior nurses immediately came over to hold her.

I placed my right hand on his chest. I said I knew how much he had gone through and that we would do our best to keep him comfortable and support him. I said that I did not think that he would die today or tomorrow, but that it would be soon. I could see him thinking about what I had said. He whispered: 'I want you all to pray with me.' He began the Our Father and by the end everyone in the room had joined. On the dresser was a beautiful icon from the Orthodox Church.

Paul looked at me and said: 'Doctor, do you think God will look after me with what I am going through? Do you think He will love me?' I answered: 'I am sure God loves you, He loves you, Paul, now and forever.'

My mouth was dry. My hand lay on his chest. My voice was barely audible and, as much to myself as to him, I repeated: 'Now and forever.'

A peace came. The nurses left the room. I stood up to leave. Paul reached for my hand along the edge of the bed and said: 'Doctor I want you to stay.' I held his hand. Paul and his mother then began a long conversation in Macedonian. Later she explained that he had tried to reassure her, settle her and talk of the mystery of God's will.

When he finished he closed his eyes and, exhausted by the encounter, fell asleep. I stood up and said slowly to his mother: 'You have a good son.'

Later I spoke with the nurses. All of us were struck by the similarity of what we had witnessed to that of another occasion. Another young man, thousands of years ago, dying in front of his mother who, turning to one of his closest friends, uttered the words: 'Comfort her.'

Frank Brennan, *Pieta*

Occasionally in the practice of palliative care, we can be pitched directly into the maelstrom of mortality. This was such an occasion. This maelstrom was made the more intense by two facts – that the patient was young and the proximity to the death of the father of the family. Grief barely dealt with was now grief compounded. Mysteries of fate and faith were tightly intertwined here.

The echoes of Calvary resonated through this encounter – the gathering of the women at the bedside, the questioning of how God will respond ('Eli, Eli: Why have you abandoned me?') and the entreaty to care for his grieving mother. The prayer, the icon, the sorrow.

* * *

Dr Frank Brennan is Catholic and a palliative care physician based in Sydney. Over time he has published narratives drawn from his work. Several have been broadcast on Australian Broadcasting Corporation (ABC) Radio National. He is also a lawyer and has written extensively on the human rights dimensions of pain management and palliative care.

Bahiyyih Nakhjavani

Bahá'i, author and teacher

FRANCE

The world beyond is as different from this world as this world is different from that of the child while still in the womb of its mother.

Bahá'u'lláh, *Gleanings from the Writings of Babá'u'lláh LXXXI*

Verily I say...the human soul is exalted above all egress and regress. It is still, and yet it soareth; it moveth, and yet it is still. It is, in itself, a testimony that beareth witness to the existence of a world that is contingent, as well as to the reality of a world that hath neither beginning nor end.

Bahá'u'lláh, *Gleanings from the Writings of Babá'u'lláh LXXXII*

I was beside my mother when she died in 2011 and I witnessed something of the passages above in experiencing that privilege. I sat there holding her hand, feeling her drifting off, floating away. I knew she did not want me to grieve in the old Persian way, although I would miss her terribly in this life. Instead, I felt as though she was giving birth to herself and I was present at the labour.

* * *

Bahiyyih Nakhjavani grew up in Iran, was raised in Africa, educated in England and America, and currently lives in France. She is a Bahá'i and author of eight books including three novels, and has been a teacher of English for over three decades (www.writingeurope.com). She is privileged at this time to be living with her distinguished father, Ali Nakhjavani.

Woris Kubo

Village elder and magistrate
PAPUA NEW GUINEA

A masked spirit dance in the Papua New Guinea Highlands
Photo: Stan Moriarty

When we die, my people believe that the spirits of the dead remain around their village. Before colonial times, the body was not buried but left on a platform to slowly decompose; only witches and lepers were buried as we feared their spirits.

We make the masks to depict the dead and use them in ceremonies called 'krina'. These ceremonies are like festivals and the masks are worn today at tribal gatherings for display. They tell stories about the dead and instruct the young to respect the spirits of the dead.

In this photograph, taken in 1966, the masked man dances boldly in front of the decorated warriors, but also weaves in and out and between them, often dancing erratically. The local villagers watch the performance intently and with great respect. Occasionally, the masked dancer darts among the villagers, hitting people and frightening the children, enforcing a respect for his spirit.

We believe that the spirits of the dead stay around the living. Sometimes they can intervene in our lives in both positive and harmful ways. It is important to have a proper farewell when someone dies, particularly for a man or woman of power or status, where we can gather together to remember and celebrate their life. We have a feast in order to keep their spirit happy.

Spirits remain in the vicinity of the village until all those they knew in life have died. Slowly the spirits then drift away, higher up into the mountains, the bush and waterfalls, where they move on to becoming spirits of the mountains and water. We forget them, and they forget us, and they cease to have any more influence over the living. (*Ol I kamap spirit bilong mountin na wara, na ol i no moa interes long ol pipel long ples. Em tasol.*)

* * *

Woris Kubo belongs to the Kamano people in the Eastern Highlands of Papua New Guinea and lives in the village of Avananofi. In his younger days he was a warrior. Today he is a village elder and magistrate. In the past, there were ceremonies where masked dancers represented the spirits of the dead. Kubo's father taught him how to make these masks, which Woris still uses in special ceremonies.

Venerable Thubten Chodron

*Tibetan Buddhist nun; Founder
and Abbess, Sravasti Abbey*

USA

The three worlds are impermanent like an autumn cloud.
The birth and death of beings is like watching a dance.
The passage of life is like lightning in the sky;
It moves quickly, like a waterfall.

Buddha, *Lalita-vistara-sūtra*

Our world and all the beings in it are transient, changing
in each successive moment, never remaining the same. Life
is unpredictable: although we want happiness, we cannot
guarantee it.

Knowing that we will all die makes us question: What is
the purpose of my life? What comes with me when I die?
At the time of death, our body, possessions, friends and
relatives, status and reputation are all left behind. We work
hard to procure and protect them while we are alive, often
at the expense of other people's happiness. Yet the energy
of our motivations and the repercussions of our actions
(karma) come with us.

Kind, generous and patient intentions and actions
lead to happiness after death; while self-centred or angry
motivations and deeds lead to painful circumstances. If we
want happiness and not pain, let's stop clinging to our stories
that blame others for our misery and misfortune. We don't
want to die with greed, hostility or resentment, so let's stop
these disturbing emotions from running our lives today.

Practising kindness, generosity and forgiveness brings happiness to ourselves and others. Having the intention to benefit others makes our lives meaningful. Let the knowledge that we will die help us to set wise priorities in life, starting now. If we do that, our death and our future lives will be more peaceful.

* * *

American-born Venerable Thubten Chodron was ordained a Tibetan Buddhist nun in 1977. She studied with His Holiness the Dalai Lama and other Tibetan masters, and is the Founder and Abbess of Sravasti Abbey, a Buddhist monastery in the USA (www.sravasti.org). She teaches Buddhism and meditation worldwide and is the author of many books including *Buddhism for Beginners* and *Working with Anger*. (www.thubtenchodron.org)

Ela Gandhi

Peace and social activist

SOUTH AFRICA

Freed from pride and delusion, having conquered attachment, dwelling ever within the Self, all desires gone, and liberated from contraries such as pleasure and pain: he of pure vision, goes to the Abode of Eternity.

Bhagavad Gita 15:5

This passage is from the Bhagavad Gita where the qualities of a good and pure human being are explained. Working at attaining this kind of purity and goodness draws one closer to God. Death is then just a way of attaining 'nirvana' or going to heaven or being one with the eternal, or God or whatever our belief.

For me, therefore, the important task is to be able to be that kind of person as described in the Gita, or in the Qur'an or in the Bible. For as Gandhiji said, 'He and His laws are one. To observe His Law is therefore the best form of worship.' Death is inevitable and a reality for which we should be prepared with dignity.

* * *

Ela Gandhi is Mahatma Gandhi's granddaughter and was born in Inanda, South Africa. Born Hindu, Ela subscribes to a universal religion. A retired social worker and peace activist, Ela is currently Trustee of the Gandhi Development Trust, Honorary President of World Conference on Religions for Peace (WCRP) and a board member of the

International Centre of Nonviolence. Ela works for the newspaper *Satyagraha*, promoting Gandhian thoughts of nonviolence.

FURTHER VERSES

We belong to God and to Him we shall return.

The Qur'an 2:156

Yea, though I walk through the valley of the shadow of death,
I will fear no evil;
For You are with me;
Your rod and staff, they comfort me.

Psalm 23:4

May the memory of the life of the departed one be for a blessing.

Jewish blessing

Death is nothing but a gateway to birth.
Nothing that lives ever dies, it only changes form.
When a man's body is weary the soul leaves
the body to receive newer and fresher garments,
And so on goes this great play of God –
from eternity to eternity.

Guru Nanak, *Graceful Exits*

Never was there a time when I did not exist nor you. Never will there be a time hereafter when any of us shall cease to be.

Bhagavad Gita 2:12

This body is not me.
I am not limited by this body.
I am life without boundaries.
I have never been born,
and I have never died.

Excerpt from Thich Nhat Hanh, *Chanting from the Heart: Buddhist Ceremonies and Daily Practices*

POSTSCRIPT
A Parable

In a mother's womb were two babies. The first baby asked the other, 'Do you believe in life after delivery?'

The second baby replied, 'Why, of course. There has to be something after delivery. Maybe we are here to prepare ourselves for what we will be later.'

'Nonsense,' said the first. 'There is no life after delivery. What would that life be?'

'I don't know, but there will be more light than here. Maybe we will walk with our legs and eat from our mouths,' said the second one.

The doubting baby laughed. 'This is absurd! Walking is impossible. And eat with our mouths? Ridiculous. The umbilical cord supplies nutrition. Life after delivery is to be excluded. The umbilical cord is too short.'

The second baby held his ground. 'I think there is something and maybe it's different than it is here.'

The first baby replied, 'No one has ever come back from there. Delivery is the end of life, and in the after-delivery it is nothing but darkness and anxiety and it takes us nowhere.'

'Well, I don't know,' said the twin, 'but certainly we will see mother and she will take care of us.'

'Mother?' The first baby guffawed. 'You believe in mother? Where is she now?'

The second baby calmly and patiently tried to explain. 'She is all around us. It is in her that we live. Without her there would not be this world.'

'Ha. I don't see her, so it's only logical that she doesn't exist,' said the first baby.

To which the other replied, 'Sometimes when you're in silence you can hear her, you can perceive her. I believe there is a reality after delivery and we are here to prepare ourselves for that reality when it comes...'

Anon

Ashgate Hospicecare

Ashgate Hospicecare, North Derbyshire (United Kingdom), is an independent registered charity that provides care to patients at its hospice, in the community and at Chesterfield Royal Hospital.

Ashgate Hospicecare opened as a purpose-built specialist palliative care unit in 1988. The hospice currently has a 21-bed inpatient unit and 16-place day hospice, and provides a range of therapy and support services on site. It also provides a wide range of community-based care and support services to enable people to stay in their own homes for as long as possible.

Ashgate Hospicecare considers that all people affected by a life-limiting illness should be treated with dignity, compassion and respect and receive the highest quality care and support – where and when they need it.

Its services are provided free of charge to patients and their families. It is funded mainly through donations, legacies and income raised through its 16 shops.

www.ashgatehospicecare.org.uk

References

Anon, 'Do not judge a song by its duration.' Accessed on 6 July 2015 at www.presentationmagazine.com/poems-for-a-young-person's-funeral-4236.htm

Anon, 'Life is a rollercoaster.' Accessed on 31 August 2015 at http://sayquotable.com/life-is-like-a-roller-coaster-it-has-its-ups-and-downs-but-its-your-choice-to-scream-or-enjoy-the-ride

Anon, 'I am not afraid of death.' Quote by Amy, an eight-year-old Norwegian girl given to the editor by an acquaintance.

Anon, 'Parable: Two babies talking in the womb...' Accessed on 24 March 2016 at http://thebacajourney.com/two-babies-talking-in-the-womb

Attributed to Seuss, T. Dr. Accessed on 17 November 2015 at http://blog.quotesome.com/10-famous-misquotations-and-misattributed-quotes

Attributed to Lao Tzu (600–531 BC) 'Life and death are one thread.' Accessed on 12 June 2015 at www.goodreads.com/quotes/3217028-life-and-death-are-one-thread-the-same-line-viewed

Attributed to Lao Tzu (600–531 BC) 'Take care with the end.' Accessed on 12 June 2015 at www.goodreads.com/quotes/117898-take-care-with-the-end-as-you-do-with-the

Saint Augustine, paraphrased from *The City of God, Book 1 Chapter 1*. (Original work written 414–426 CE.) Accessed on 26 May 2015 at www.catholicculture.org/culture/library/fathers/view.cfm?recnum=3274

Baal Shem Tov, I. (1698–1760) 'Forgetfulness leads to exile and remembering is the key to redemption.' Accessed on 12 June 2015 at www.myjewishlearning.com/article/the-importance-of-remembering

Bahá'u'lláh, *Gleanings from the Writings of Bahá'u'lláh, LXXXI and LXXXII.* Translated by Shoghi Effendi, US Baha'i Publishing Trust 1990 (Original first edition published in 1935) Accessed on 1 June 2016 at http://reference.bahai.org/en/t/o/BNE/bne-153.html; http://reference.bahai.org/en/t/b/GWB/gwb-82.html

Beecher, L.F. (1903) 'What is Dying?' Accessed on 24 November 2015 at http://blog.transylvaniandutch.com/2013/01/poetry-friday-what-is-dying-luther-f.html

Saint Benedict, 'The instrument of good works, Rule 47' in *The Rule of Benedict.* (Original work written in the sixth century). Accessed on 12 June 2015 at www.osb.org/rb/text/rbejms2.html#4

Bhagavad Gita 2:12, translated from the Sanskrit by Swami Nikhilananda of the Ramakrishna Vivekananda Center, New York. (Original work dated 400–300 BC.)

Bhagavad Gita 2:22–23, translated by Dr Pushpa Bhardwaj-Wood. (Original work dated 400–300 BC.)

Bhagavad Gita 15:5, translated by Dr S. Radhakrishnan. Selected Shlokas set to music by Vanraj Bhatia. New Delhi: Aroon Purie Living Media India Ltd. (Original work dated 400–300 BC.)

The Bible, Psalm 23:4, New King James Version.

The Bible, Isaiah 41:10; 42:6, New Revised Standard Version.

The Bible, Isaiah 64:8, New Revised Standard Version.

The Bible, Ecclesiastes 3:1, King James Bible.

The Bible, Ecclesiastes 3:7, New International Version.

The Bible, Ecclesiastes 12:7, The World English Bible.

The Bible, John 1:5, New American Standard Bible.

The Bible, 2 Corinthians 4:16, King James Bible.

Borges. J.L. (2000) 'Elegy for a park' in Alexander Coleman (ed.) *Jorge Luis Borges: Selected Poems.* Translated by A. Reid, M. Kodama, W. Barnstone, A. Coleman *et al.* New York: Penguin Random House.

Brennan, F. *(2009)* 'Pieta' in *Standing on the Platform: Stories and Reflections from Palliative Care.* Self-published by Vision Media.

Buddha, Tsong-kha-pa (2015) 'Lalita-vistara-sūtra' in *The Great Treatise on the Stages of the Path to Enlightenment, Volume 1,* edited by J. Cutler and G. Newland, translated by Lamrim Chenmo Translation Committee. Boston, MA: Shambhala Publications. (Completed in 1402, based on classical Indian Buddhist literature.)

Bunyan, J. (1953) *The Pilgrim's Progress,* edited by G.F. Maine. London: Collins. (Original work published in 1678.)

Carver, R. (1989) 'Late fragment' in *All of Us*. London: Harvill Press.

Celtic Blessing, 'I lay my head to rest.' Blessing given to Su Chard by a fellow celebrant.

Celtic Blessing, 'May the gentleness of the water.' Accessed on 26 June 2015 at www.clarelibrary.ie/eolas/cominfo/arts/A_time_to_remember.pdf

Chief White Elk (Oto Nation), 'When you were born, you cried.' Accessed on 20 November 2015 at www.quotes-motivational.com/Motivational/Spiritual-Quotes.html

Dasgupta, A. *Once upon a Star*. Unpublished.

de Chardin, P.T. (1966) *Le Milieu Divin (The Divine Milieu)*. Paris: Editions du Seuil. (Original work written in 1926–7; first published in 1957; first published in English in 1960).

de Hennezel, M. (1995) *Intimate Death: How the Dying Teach Us to Live*, translated by Christopher Thiéry (preface), Carol Brown Janeway. Paris: Robert Laffont, SA.

de Mello, A. (1984) 'The Salt Doll' in *The Song of the Bird*. New York: Image Books. (Original work published in 1981.)

de Montaigne, M. (1991) *The Complete Essays*, translated by M.A. Screech. London: Allen Lane The Penguin Press, Penguin Classics 1993. (Original version published in 1580.)

Donne, J. 'Death, be not proud' [excerpt]. In *Holy Sonnet 10*. (Original work published in 1633.) Accessed on 31 August 2015 at www.poetryfoundation.org/poem/173363

Donne, J. 'No man is an island' [excerpt from Meditation 17]. *Devotions upon Emergent Occasions*. (Original work published in 1624.) Accessed on 31 August 2015 at www.poemhunter.com/poem/no-man-is-an-island

Drayton, L. (2004) 'Thank you', Track 13. From the album *Bliss* by Bliss. www.lucindadrayton.com

Duffy, C.A. (2009) [excerpt] *Last Post*. (Dame Carol Ann Duffy, Poet Laureate of the UK, wrote *Last Post* to mark the deaths of Henry Allingham and Harry Patch, the two longest surviving soldiers from the First World War. It was first broadcast on BBC Radio on 30 July 2009, the day of Allingham's funeral.)

Eliot, T.S. (1944) 'Little Gidding' [excerpt] in *Four Quartets*. London: Faber and Faber.

Frankl, V.E. (1992) *Man's Search for Meaning*. Boston, MA: Beacon Press. (Original work published in 1959.)

Gandhi, M.K. *Young India* (editions: 2 February 1922; 12 March 1930). Accessed on 7 April 2016 at www.gandhiheritageportal.org

Garrett, S.L. (2013) *When Death Speaks*. Victoria, BC: Friesen Press.

Gawler, I. (2013) 'The clear moment of death' in *You Can Conquer Cancer*. Melbourne: Michelle Anderson Publishing. (Original work published in 1984.)

Gibran, K. *The Prophet*. Penguin Random House/Estate. (Original work published in 1923.)

Gissing, V. (1988) *Pearls of Childhood*. London: Robson Books.

Green, J. (2006) *An Abundance of Katherines*. New York: Penguin.

Guru Nanak in *Graceful Exits* (1997) Sushila Blackman (ed) Boston: Shambhala Publications. wwww.shambhala.com

Hammarskjöld, D. (1964) *Markings*, translated by L. Sjöberg and W.H. Auden. London: Faber & Faber.

Hardy, T. (1917) 'Afterwards' in *Moments of Vision and Miscellaneous Verses*. London: McMillan.

Harkins, D. (1981) 'Remember Me.' Poem read at the Queen Mother's funeral on Tuesday 9 April 2002, titled *She is Gone*. Accessed on 18 June 2015 at www.poeticexpressions.co.uk/poems/you%20can%20shed%20tears%20that%20she%20is%20gone.htm

Hoffman, Y. (1986) *Japanese Death Poems*. Tokyo: Charles E. Tuttle Inc.

Jewish proverb, 'The body is the garden of the soul.'

Jewish blessing, 'May the memory of the life of the departed one be for a blessing.'

Kemp, R. *Everyone a Hero* [excerpt]. Message given at Andrew Griffiths' memorial service.

Kiser, J. (2003) *The Monks of Tibhirine: Faith, Love, and Terror in Algeria*. New York: St Martin's Griffin.

Kitzinger, S. (1983) *Women's Experience of Sex*. London: Dorling Kindersley.

Kushner, H.S. (2002) *When Bad Things Happen to Good People*. London: Pan Books. (Original work published in 1981.)

Machado, A. (2003) 'There is no road' in *There is No Road*, translated by M. Berg and D. Maloney. Buffalo, NY: White Pine Press. (Original work published 1917.)

Mariner, R. (2009) *Movement for Reform Judaism (MRJ) Funeral Service Book*.

Medieval prayer. Accessed on 21 December 2015 at www.rcwms.org/resources/SOG/2011_12_newsletter.pdf

Mendel, M., Rabbi of Rymanov (2002) 'Human beings are God's language' in preface H.S. Kushner, *When Bad Things Happen to Good People*. London: Pan Books.

Native American Prayer. It is likely that this has been adapted by person(s) unknown from the original poem 'Do not stand at my grave and weep', generally attributed to Mary Frye, 1932. Accessed on 3 August 2015 at www.businessballs.com/donotstandatmygraveandweep.htm

Neruda, P. (1975) 'Death Alone' [excerpt] in *Selected Poems*. Edited by Nathaniel Tarn, translated by A. Kerrigan, W.S. Merlin and N. Tarn. London: Penguin Random House. (Original work published in 1935.)

Nhat Hanh, T. (2007) 'Contemplation on No-Coming and No-Going' in *Chanting from the Heart: Buddhist Ceremonies and Daily Practices*, Berkeley, CA: Parallax Press.

O'Donohue, J. (2007) 'For the dying' [excerpt] in *Benedictus – A Book of Blessings*. London: Bantam Press.

O'Donohue, J. (2007) 'Blessing: For the dying' [excerpt] in *To Bless the Space Between Us: A Book of Blessings*. London: Bantam Press.

O'Donohue, J. and Quinn, J. (2015) *Walking on the Pastures of Wonder – John O'Donohue in conversation with John Quinn*. Dublin: Veritas.

Oliver, M. (2009) 'Mysteries, Yes' in *Evidence*. Boston: Beacon Press.

The Qur'an 1:1–7 Al Fatihah, translated by Abdullah Yusuf Ali (1934).

The Qur'an 2:156, translated by M.A.S. Abdel Haleem (2004).

Richardson, I.P. (1943) 'To Those I Love.' Accessed on 24 September 2015 at www.qingming.com/resources/poem.htm

Rilke, R.M. (1996) *Rilke's Book of Hours: Love Poems to God*, translated by A. Barrows and J. Macy. New York: Riverhead Books. (Original work published in 1905.)

Rinpoche, S. (1998) *The Tibetan Book of Living and Dying*. San Francisco: Harper San Francisco. (Original work published in 1992.)

Rinpoche, Lama Zopa (1999) Transcript of teachings of Lama Zopa Rinpoche, Vajrasattva retreat, Land of Medicine Buddha, California.

Roosevelt, T. (1910) 'The man in the arena' in *Citizenship in a Republic* speech, Sorbonne, Paris. Accessed on 12 June 2015, www.theodore-roosevelt.com/trsorbonnespeech.html

Rumi, M.J. Inscription on Rumi's shrine. Translated by Coleman Barks. Used with permission. Accessed on 11 June 2015 at www.goodreads.com/quotes/79822-come-come-whoever-you-are-wanderer-worshiper-lover-of-leaving

Schoenbeck, S.L. (2011) *Good Grief: Daily Meditations: A Book of Caring and Remembrance*. Newport, OR: Dancing Moon Press.

Shakespeare, W. *Hamlet*, Act 1, Scene 2.

Shawiak, R.V. 'Aspects of Death.' Accessed on 11 June 2015 at www.poemhunter.com/poem/aspects-of-death

Shine, P. (1995) *Yurrandaali Dreaming: A Collection of Stories and Poems*. Unpublished.

Sri Guru Granth Sahib Ji. Sri Guru Granth Sahib is the holy scripture of the Sikh faith. The selections presented here were translated by *Bhai Sahib Bhai (Dr) Mohinder Singh Ahluwalia*.

Stevenson, R.L. (1913) 'Where go the boats?' in *A Child's Garden of Verses*. London: Simon & Schuster. (Original work published in 1885.)

Tagore, R. *Epigraph*. Accessed on 24 November 2015 at www.quotationspage.com/quote/32486.html

Thomas, D. (2014) 'Do not go gentle into that good night' in *The Collected Poems of Dylan Thomas: The New Centenary Edition*. London: Orion. (Original work published in 1951.)

Contributor Index